I0015109

ITIL® v4 Complete Certification Guidebook

Study Guide to Pass In First Attempt

Jaden Locus

ITIL® - ITIL® is a (registered) Trade Mark of AXELOS Limited. All rights reserved.

Contents

If you are willing to apply for the ITIL 4 Foundation Certification test, then this guide will help you to obtain maximum benefits by providing all the necessary details and information regarding this particular exam. This manuscript is going to help you learn everything essential to pass the Information Technology Infrastructure Library (ITIL®) 4 Foundation test if you are applying for the first time. Moreover, the overall ITIL 4 infrastructure will be visible to you so that you can use and apply it in your own business. It's a famous saying that you cannot get a full understanding of any subject until you don't get your hands dirty on it. So this is going to be an excellent platform for beginners whether you are going to grab information about the ITIL 4 framework or you want to get prepared for the ITIL 4 foundation test. This idea means that it can benefit you in either two ways: you can get promotion to a higher rank in your organization, or you can switch to an entirely new job. Every concept of the actual ITIL 4 Foundation textbook has included in this book, which explicitly aimed to teach you everything without the need to read a real manual. Before starting the lesson of this book, I would like to give a brief introduction to Information Technology Infrastructure library because not every individual has much knowledge about this lesson or why we use it. ***ITIL is a service management framework.*** *The term 'Service Management' refers to a specific set of business proficiencies and abilities that facilitates the clients of that particular organization by providing IT services.* The ITIL framework is used for this purpose to provide a complete framework by managing IT services for the businesses of large companies efficiently.

The worldwide demand for ITIL has been increased in the last previous decades because it is considered to be a very effective and useful framework for IT Service Management all over the globe. It has now gained popularity and has become the most popular service management framework. The reason behind its popularity is that most of the big enterprises in the entire world uses and manages their IT management setups with the help of the ITIL framework. The short form of this term is ITSM, i.e., IT Service Management. IT Service Management plays a vital role in the IT administration system of an organization. The IT Infrastructure Library (ITIL) is the most useful and practical system for applying ITSM. It is essential to comprehend the advantages that ITIL procedures can bring to any business with the emerging need for such services globally. It was anticipated that most of the large firms want to take the advantages of utilizing ITIL frameworks because IT Infrastructure Library (ITIL) gives guiding principles to IT facility providers on how to configure, accomplish and support IT administrations. ITIL is the most generally utilized IT administration facility. You can see best practices of ITIL on the internet that can use in executing the processes of service support.

Usually, the Service Management of a particular organization has the responsibility of producing and looking after the service packages and service supply frameworks that satisfy client needs and the powerful and proficient supervision of the day-to-day tasks in the respective company. Thus, it is the objective of the Service Management team to provide quality assurance service so that it meets the client demands as well as satisfaction, inside the company's business means and is dependent on a Service Culture which organizations view as an essential for conveying quality products. There is a direct connection exists between the satisfaction of the consumer and the utilization of ITIL. Also, Customer Satisfaction indicates that the services provisions of a particular organization are beneficial. This concept should be in your mind that both consumer satisfaction and operational throughput are directly proportional to the ITIL structure. Client satisfaction, as well as operational throughput increases as the exercises in the ITIL system increases. If the use of ITIL structure has increased due to some reasons, then it would bring out the positive effects on consumer satisfaction and operational throughput. Thus, making a direct relationship between these three crucial factors. This concept is essential for large enterprises while applying ITIL frameworks. It is a brief introduction of the ITIL framework so that any individual, who does not have any knowledge ITIL frameworks, can easily understand its core concepts for IT service management of large firms. You must be wondering what this introduction is getting too long and when you will get all the essential tips for the Foundation test. Well, don't worry; we are now directly jumping into the section of exam fundamentals where you can get all the information regarding ITIL Foundation Test, how to apply for it and how you can pass the test with this book in no time.

Exams Fundamentals

In this section, we are going to discuss the details of the ITIL 4 Foundation test. If you are a student applying for the test, then you must be taking this lesson for the one reason, i.e., you want to become ITIL 4 certified. And if you are a full-time worker who needs this certification to get promotion in your current organization or maybe you haven't got any job, and you need this certification to get one in the Information Technology sector. No matter what the cause is, the lesson in this book was designed in such a way that anyone could get the desirable knowledge related to ITIL 4. This lesson is going to provide the material you need to know so that you can pass the foundation test and help you focus on the studies. The very first step in this process is to understand how the ITIL 4 test has designed before getting yourselves engaged in the depth of the book. Your capability to comprehend or memorize the concepts from this book can help you crack the questions in the exam. The two keywords I have used here 'comprehend' and 'memorize' should be noted. Let's say a problem in the exam requires your ability to memorize a concept and recalling it. Then this means that you must be capable enough to point out the correct definition from the given multiple choices in the exam. For example, we have studied the service management concept in the book, and a question asked in the paper is related to the definition of service management. The description in the problem is the same as the definition we have used in the book. You have been given four different terms for that specific definition; then, you have to select the best suitable name among four options that match the given description. Presently, this is the case of a recall or memorize difficulty level in the exam. In the test, there will be nine questions viewed as recall questions. Hence, it's vital to keep these definitions in your mind and remember them that we provide in this book. These definitions are available to you in the downloadable guide.

Let's discuss the second key term 'comprehend' that I have used in the above passage. If a question in the exam comes from a portion of what we call 'comprehend' which means that it requires your ability to understand something, then you must be capable enough to describe the definition of a concept or a term based on the choices given. It surely doesn't mean that you need to write the word to word. Instead, you may provide some examples, and the question asks you to select the best ITIL term or concept related to the example. A suitable name should be selected that best matches the example. With the help of this book, you will be able to learn all the ITIL 4 main concepts and can answer the questions asked in the exam without a lot of trouble only if you are fully devoted to this book. At this stage, you must be thinking about how would you take the ITIL 4 certification exam and become certified? The good news is, unlike other certification exams, you can give this ITIL 4 certification test online while being in your comfort zone. You can go on the PoepleCert website or any other valid site to get yourself registered. To plan your test, you do require a test voucher; however, the fact that this takes care of the expense of the test itself. You can purchase the test voucher from PeopleCert on their site at $349 cost, or you can go to any other website that is offering the same certification test. Once you get your voucher, you would then be able to plan your test date and timings since you gathered information on the key terms 'comprehension' and 'memorization' used in the foundation exam. Where to purchase your voucher, and how to plan your test, what is the next step? We should now discuss the test itself.

There are some key statistical data points that you have to keep mind. Firstly, the test is planned. You will get an hour for the entire test. In case you're not a local English speaker, however, you're taking the test in English, you can feel free to get an additional 15 minutes on the test if you demand it during your schedule arrangements. It is going to help you a lot as it will increase your time up to 75 minutes if you demand extra time. Presently, for us all English speakers, however, we just get an hour. Try not to stress; however, an hour is a lot of time for this test. A large portion of students finishes in around 30 minutes. There are 40 multiple choice questions in the foundation test like A, B, C, or D options, and you have to select one best answer. It means that you do not need in-depth (very detailed) comprehension and word for word memorization of ITIL 4 concepts to crack the test. You just need to be familiar with a simple level of understanding and memorization, and that's the key to pass the test. So the passing percentage required for the ITIL 4 certification test is 65% or above and to get the certificate. Which makes it 26 correct questions out of 40 questions. You have to answer at least 26 right questions. And to prepare you for the test, it is recommended to take the sample or practice tests before attempting the actual test. It will let you know where you stand in terms of your knowledge. If you require more tests to practice, then you should take the quiz questions available online.

At the point when you're taking a training test, I prescribe going for 75% or higher to think of it as a pass since this will give you a 10% security that if you wind up having a terrible test day or you get anxious when giving the actual test. It's just because each time you give the test, you need to purchase another voucher, and you just need to take it once. I've said that you will get 40 multiple choice questions on test day, yet they are comprised of three different kinds of questions. These multiple-choice questions are Classic questions, Missing word, and the last one List. We are discussing each kind of these questions here. Let's take the example of a classic question. For example, who is the founder (CEO) of Facebook? A. Steve Jobs, B. Mark Zuckerburg, C. Andy Jassy, or D. Walt Disney? So if you are a Facebook user (probably more than half of the world uses it), then you must have heard the name of Mark Zuckerburg. Such types of questions are known as a negative classic, which is being asked in the test. That is represented by the word that does not exist in the question statement. So if the question statement is: which is not the name of Big Tech companies in the world? A. Apple, B. Microsoft, C. Kfc, or D. IBM? You can clearly distinguish between a food company (i.e., Kfc here) and a tech company. SO the right answer is C., Kfc is a very popular fast food service provider, and the other three are big tech companies. The second type of question in the exam is called a missing word. It is usually shown by '?' that shows one word or short phrase of 2, 3, or 4 words. Let's take a simple example: A _____ is a vegetable type? A. Apple, B. Banana, C. Grapes, or D. Carrot? You know that Carrot is the type of vegetable, and the other three are fruits. So, in the exam, you have to put the right answer in the blank area to check whether it makes sense or not. And then select the option in the multiple-choice questions. The last kind of question you can expect to come to the exam is a list question. There are no more than two or three questions like these in the exam. In the list questions, there is more than one right answer. There is a numbered list, and you have to select multiple options according to the question statement. For example, which are the five senses of the human body? One. Ear, Nose and tongue, Two. Brain, Three. Eyes & skin or Four, heart. Well, everyone knows that the human body has five sensing organs that are ear, nonsense, tongue, eyes, and skin. So, the options one and three would select in this case. You have to look for the options that correspond with the question statement. After all the details about the ITIL 4 foundation test, everything should be clear to you. Let's focus on the lesson now.

Service Organizations

Remember the time of your childhood when you joined the school; you may have come across the term 'Industrial Revolution.' It was the first time in centuries that an industrial revolution took place. You have taught that the first industrial revolution happened in the eighteenth and nineteenth centuries most across the USA and Europe. At that time, mankind moved from an agricultural-based, rural society associated with farmers into an urbanized industrial region that later formed into our nation's biggest communities. This specific movement gave rise to the growth and expansion of automation as textile and iron industries just as the benefits of the steam motor for our transportation needs. The Industrial Revolution was just the first; however, mankind moved into the Second Industrial Revolution at the end of the nineteenth century and proceeding into the First World War. During this period, our businesses extended to incorporate steel, oil, power, an addition to electrically fueled equipment to assist in the large scale manufacturing of products. The vehicle industry was also developed with the invention of internal combustion engines in the cars due to which traveling and transport services became significantly effective. Simultaneously, candle lights are being replaced with electric light bulbs, enabling us to work longer into the night as compared to the previous days when there was no such facility. Furthermore, the invention of the telephone was not less than a miracle, which made it possible for humans to communicate over long distances. Life could not have been much better than before; however, mankind wasn't finished investigating and discovering things yet.

Because of the growing demand and benefits, technology was continuously progressing, but there were not any big innovations that happened until the end of the twentieth century. The technology suddenly started to evolve tremendously around 1980, and a real major change occurred in the history of the world in the form of the digital revolution. The digital revolution was the Third Industrial Revolution, which was way more advanced than the second revolution. When it began, the microchip computer technology has been developed, which contains analog as well as digital electronics. This technology completely changed the lives of humans because humans started to use this technology in their daily life activities such as PCs, the Internet, and a wide range of technologies for information and communication. Thus, it became one of the essential parts of the human race. The technologies of this time are still in use of the organizations, but they have gone very much advanced nowadays. It was the time when ITIL first formed during the third Industrial Revolution. ITIL was initially created to provide directions and guidelines in the best way possible for the information technology organizations to run effectively. ITIL, as it was initially created, was an abbreviation that represented *the Information Technology Infrastructure Library.* ITIL started during the 1980s as a path for associations to make procedures and methods to more effectively run their Information Technology frameworks. Thus, ITIL turned into the existing standard all around the globe for the service management of IT systems, in the last three decades.

As a human society, we moved from the 1st Industrial Revolution to the second, and afterward, on to the third, we're currently at a junction once more. Presently, we're getting into the fourth Industrial Revolution, and it is going on the present moment. The production of virtual physical frameworks has been evolving in the Fourth Industrial Revolution. In which different technologies are being combined and burring the outlines between physical and computerized domains. This revolution utilizes artificial intelligence technology, the Internet of things, mechanical technology, Nano innovation, and self-governing vehicles, thus significantly more. This mind-blowing development in innovation in the mid 21st century has completely changed our world as well as ourselves. Things being what they are, you might be thinking at this moment, why on earth we are investing our energy into discussing the historical backdrop of different Industrial Revolutions that happened in the lesson of the last hundred years? Well, I have directed you to come to this meaningful conclusion. Information Technology Infrastructure Library (ITIL) Four isn't its fourth version. Rather, it is ITIL of the fourth Industrial Revolution. ITIL is a brand name, not to be considered as an abbreviation anymore. It implies ITIL that doesn't mean Information Technology Infrastructure Library any longer since ITIL is something other than just infrastructure. It is considered to be a significant move in the manner that ITIL approaches and tackles the hurdles of IT service management dependent on this too.

Service Management

In the previous segment of the book, I have discussed the key point that ITIL is a detailed infrastructure for the service management of IT systems, also known as ITSM. According to this ITIL 4, the definition of *Service Management refers to the set of expert organizational abilities and proficiencies which facilitate clients with their services in the best way possible to ensure value to clients.* As we are talking about organizational abilities in the context of service management, this means that such organizations have a high level of proficiencies that they can perform all the functions necessary to provide the best service management. Now, if you want to carry out the best service management with the help of the ITIL 4 framework or any other framework of IT service management within your organization, and your entire focus is on to provide the best customer value and facilitate them with the preferred benefits. For this purpose, a company should bring together its employees to help the company's activities, practices, and procedures in the best way possible. Such exercises, practices, and procedures are like a motor engine that energies the production of the company's items and their customer services. But, none of these exercises, practices, and procedures can be possible in disconnection. Therefore, the relationships that are made, raised, and supported all through the process of Service Management, are necessary.

In this segment of the book, we will talk about these basic ideas of Service Management that are used with the ITIL 4 framework as well as other infrastructures. After that, we will be going over the ideas of results(outcomes), dangers, utility, and guarantee to help you form a strong base before we dive into the major concepts of ITIL 4 that are discussed in detail in more than half a portion of this book. Even though the core ideas in this segment are combined for IT Service Management, that doesn't mean they won't be on the ITIL 4 test. We're going to cover every one of the three pieces of learning Objective A1, in this segment of the book. This incorporates learning Objective 1.1, which says that you will just have to review (memorize) the description of utility, service, guarantee, user, client, service management, and sponsor. You can probably get two multiple choice questions from this Learning Objective on your confirmation test. In this segment of objective 1.2, you will be required to depict the ideas of cost, organization, value, result, hazard, utility, and guarantee. On your test, two MCQs will come from this specific Learning Objective too.

At last, we will also be learning Objective 1.3, which expects you to demonstrate the key ideas of service relationships, including service contributions, service relationship management, delivery, and utilization of services. In the test, you can hope to get one inquiry from this specific Learning Objective. Thus, we should begin the topic of Service Management and its fundamental ideas.

Value

You must be wondering what this term 'value' means here? Well, in the framework of ITIL 4, the *term value refers to perceived profits, efficacy, and worth of anything.* Yeah, I know that the term is very common, but let's find out its meaning in the context of service management. The concept of value is essential when it comes to ITIL 4 framework as well as service management. First of all, focus on this short definition of value that it is interpreted or perceived. *This implies that the significant worth of something is always abstract.* Now, who gets the chance to decide this apparent measure of value? The benefit is saved for the receiver of the value, i.e., a customer who receives the value. Give me a chance to help you explain it better. Let's suppose there are two flatmates, Ana and Maria. One evening, the two of them decide that they want to drink flavored milk. They stroll over to the fridge to get themselves bottles of flavored milk and find out that there's just one remaining in the fridge. They start to fight with one another that every individual truly needs that milk bottle for themselves. Ana says she values the milk bottle more, and she ought to have it, yet Maria rapidly answers that she values it more and that she ought to have it. Neither one of the persons discloses to the next why they need the milk bottle. Rather, they don't let them know of the worth they see that it has. In any case, being the storyteller, I know precisely what every one of them needs to do with that flavored milk.

Ana is starving, so she wanted to have a sweet and healthy liquor. If she gets a chance to take the flavored milk bottle, she intends to drink the milk from the bottle and discard the bottle. In her apparent value of this milk bottle, the inside of the milk bottle contains 100% of the worth, and the bottle itself is trash. It is useless. While on the other hand, Maria is a creative designer who makes beautiful things from trash. This evening, she wanted to make some designs. She needed the milk bottle that looks beautiful to her for her new designs. In case, if she gets the milk bottle, she intends just to utilize the bottle and throw away the flavored milk into the waste bin as she does not have the intention to drink it. Not like Ana, who places 100% of the milk's worth on its capacity to be gulped up, Maria thinks that the milk inside the bottle is useless. Instead, she puts 100% of the value into the bottle of flavored milk. I'm certain you can see the intriguing fact here about worth. This one milk bottle could serve 100% of the requirements for every individual in this example, only if they could talk about their actual wishes for that milk bottle. They could have 100% of the worth of milk bottles because the end recipient sees the worth. For this situation, both Ana and Maria, each interpret it differently. To the shopkeeper, who is the first provider of this milk bottle, he sold the milk bottle for just two dollars. How would you tell that the two of them esteemed that $2 milk bottle for different reasons? Possibly the shopkeeper would have changed the bottle and pour the milk in a low-quality bottle and sold the bottle and milk separately for $2. What if he had done such thing to both flatmates, he would have multiplied the value of milk bottle for himself? I realize that sounds somewhat insane; however, I bet on test day you will recall about this milk bottle and value.

You will be memorizing this concept that the amount of value that something has depends on the recipient's view of that worth. The recipient requires to get the value from items, relationships, from the services, from whatever it is that we're hoping to supply or to provide the value for them. Due to this reason, the term value is always viewed as abstract, and it may be not quite the same as what the original seller intended for. It might be unique with what they had defined the item as or what facility it would offer, and from what we initially settled to. This subjectivity must be caught, estimated, and calculated because this is the thing that we need to work within a service management organization. How about we return to our meaning of value again. It is the perceived profits, efficacy, and worth of anything. As I said previously, this definition is somewhat conventional because it utilizes this indefinite term of something. The makers of ITIL explicitly picked the term 'value' because service management is way more than just services nowadays because the perceived profits and efficacy of something truly rely upon the discussion of the situation.

In each given situation, we have the idea of what that something is, and we realize what it implies in the definition of value. But in a common definition like this, we can't just run down everything something can be, so something turns into that placeholder. Since when we talk about worth, it is truly dependent on these connections too. We will examine those service connections in an upcoming exercise.

Organizations and people

As we are talking about organization, it does not mean that it is constrained to a specific supplier or an information technology department of a company or even a large IT service management organization. Rather, we're simply considering it as a standard organization that delivers the best services to customers. Whereas, the customer is a character performed by association that utilizes those services and gets benefits from them. There are many types of organizations that vary in sizes as well as complexity. And, some organizations also fluctuate in their legal structure in that they are solitary individuals, a group, or even a large international enterprise. What truly limits an association together is a set of common goals, affairs, and authorities. This may appear to be abnormal in the case of an individual who can serve as an organization; however, it truly works along with these concepts in reality. At the point when a person forms a company, it is made as sole ownership initially. Such companies have just a single person who is working as an associate in all business affairs.

But most of the time, an enterprise is a group of individuals moving in the direction of a common goal to achieve it together. As any small organization grows bigger and bigger, they hire a large number of groups of individuals, which make up several small associations inside the organization. There is a training group in organizations that experts lead, and there is also an operations team that is led by operations head. It is a case of how individuals are organized in a coordinated manner to work for shared objectives and to accomplish them inside a big business association. In the majority of these cases, the common goals are generally those targets that give value to customers, but how the worth is attained, has changed in ITIL 4 framework. Before that, we view value as something that conveyed from supplier to client of the service; however, this wasn't the precise case in reality. People say that Conveying something is simple; however, conveying something of value is hard. Still, it was so inappropriate, and it started to uprise all over the IT service management trade. Therefore, ITIL 4 acknowledges that worth must be co-created by the supplier and the customer. What does this mean for us in reality? Let's consider this lesson or any lesson online, for instance. I have invested a great amount of energy writing and publishing this lesson so you could get an advantage from it. Also, I am sure that this is the best book you can get your hands on. And I placed a great deal of significant worth on the content of the book, and I hope that you can get benefit from it. How about we take this book from your viewpoint as the customer. Is this manuscript worth it?

You have come here to get knowledge of the ITIL 4 and certification exam, so you probably feel that this book has some value; otherwise, you wouldn't have come to read it. In case you are a student, you likely are going to check whether this book sufficiently makes you ready for passing percentage in the exam or not. In any case, we need to co-create the worth together so that you can accomplish that ideal value and pass the test. Let's discuss another example to help you understand this concept deeply. Let's suppose I am the owner of a company of electric cars and you are a customer who wants to buy a new model car. I have shown you two new models of Tesla Model 3 and Model S. They are the fastest electric cars of this time. So, as a supplier, I have showcased my best vehicles for you. Whereas, as a customer, you state your requirements for the new car. You explain the qualities of the desired car that the new model must possess. You need a car that must have the option to drive autonomously. You need a vehicle that can travel 150 miles/hour before it should be recharged or any sort of other requirements. Now the last condition you express is that you need a beautiful model, but it should also be cost-effective. It is the place where things originated from a cost perspective, and thus, this is considered as your third job role as sponsor. You say I may like the Model S, and it sells for nearly $150,000. Will Model 3 still meet all the client's needs, although it sells for just 70,000? If this is the case, then the sponsor in you would prefer to pick the more affordable Model. So, when you are going to get a new car, you're genuinely considering these roles inside your mind before buying anything.

Let's take the same example in a different case. Suppose that you are going to purchase a new car for another person. In this case, you are buying a new car for your daughter. She is near to the age where she is mature enough to drive the car, as she is the customer in this situation. Since she needs her parents to get her first new car, so it doesn't matter to her the amount it costs. She also doesn't have any requirements; all she wants to use the asset and needs to be able to get in and drive from one location to another. For this situation, this implies she can drive anywhere she needs, and she'll have the option to drive whatever her parents choose to purchase for her. You will be our client again. You're going to set the requirements for the new care your daughter wants, and this service needs to meet those prerequisites, and you are the one who takes your daughter's responsibility for driving this car. When your daughter drives that car, you are going to take responsibility for anything that happens because she is my client in this case. You may create any requirement for this car as you're buying it for your daughter. Let's say your daughter demands a car that has four seats in it; thus, it must have four doors. The vehicle might have driver and traveler airbags in it.

Also, the desired car must have to be less than five years old. It is the specific requirement from your daughter that car can be second-hand (already used), but it shouldn't be used for more than five years and so on. Your daughter can demand any requirement according to her needs because she is the customer, and she has that right as well as ability. As we discussed the third role of a person as a customer, i.e., sponsor, and this person is paying for the car. The sponsor may be a different person in many cases. But, in this case, you're also acting as a sponsor. As you are the one who is buying a car for your daughter, so, you need to decide the budget for the car which you can easily afford. You have to pay for this car in this case. Let's say that you have a budget of a maximum of $20,000, and as a customer, you can pick any car that you need for your daughter, but it has to be in the same budget that you created. So, it means that you can't buy a new model car whether you may want to buy it for your beloved daughter or she may want it. So, you act as a customer who buys this service, whereas your daughter acts as a service user. You have created a specific budget to buy this car, and you have to be in that budget. Therefore, this sort of thing usually takes place in businesses most of the time. In some businesses, you have to act as one of these job roles relying upon the situation. Sometimes you have to act as one role in some businesses while, in some cases, you have to act as two or, all three roles in the critical business deals. For instance, you want to buy specific software that your business team needs to work for your regular client. Now, you define the requirements that your team wants, and you also have the right to assign and approve the budget for those requirements. In this particular case, you are acting as both the client and the sponsor, whereas, your business team will act as users because they are going to use the software that you purchase.

You must be in a great position when you act as both the customer and the sponsor because you are in charge of approving the budget as well as you have the authority to decide the desired requirements. However, in the case of large enterprises, the employee who approves the budget for specific IT services is neither the client not the user of that service, and this sort of detachment can create issues. The reason for these issues is that the sponsor who pays for the requirements, and the client who makes those requirements that best suit their needs, usually argue on making such demands. Both of them have different perspectives in their heads because one focuses on cost-effective funds, while others entirely focus on the requirements and its usage. The key point to be noted here is that there is a slight difference between the customer and the user of the service because customers create demands for the service while users are only concerned about using the service. This problem also affects the interest of the user and the customer. Therefore, a service provider must identify these three roles on a client-side so that all of them receive the best delivery and right services according to their requirements. Thus, as a service provider, we need to ensure that the sponsor makes the cost-effective budget, which, in return, meets the customer's requirement, and the user gets the satisfaction of our services. In the end, our main goal is to make client, user and sponsor satisfied so that when all of the three meet up, we undoubtedly get more orders for our services from the customer's organization.

Services and Products

One of the main reasons for creating ITIL 4 is to lead the service management inside global enterprises. Thus, we have a particular meaning of what we call 'service' in our business organizations. So, the term service refers to ***the methods of enabling co-created value to facilitate the client's desired results, with the security that the client wouldn't have to deal with the expenses and threats***. This term is defined in the light of the ITIL 4 framework, and you need to be able to understand this definition and memorize it for the exam. Therefore, we are going to divide this definition into chunks and discuss it one piece at a time. Let's take the first portion of the definition that service is the method of enabling co-created value. This specific part says that value is obtained in the result of connecting the service provider and service user. The next part of the definition states that this relationship is made by facilitating the client's desired results. Once again, this topic explanation returns to the idea of value. In case I'm providing you something like a service provider, then, unless it doesn't have any worth, it's not going to help you as the client to fulfill your requirements. So, taking the examples of value, we discussed earlier, if it doesn't assist you in passing your test, then the worth of this book is not co-created. But you can't expect the service provider to accomplish your goals for you, and you need to accomplish them yourself. The facilitator's job is to simplify the accomplishment of those client results. So, if you want to pass the certification test, I can only deliver the required material and steps to attempt the test. But, you have to study and learn it all on your own. The same goes for the IT service provider. I can guarantee you that your PC is up and ready to run a program, yet you don't give the essential inputs to that program, you won't get the desired results you want.

Now, the last portion of the definition expresses that the co-created value is made with the security that the client wouldn't have to deal with the extra expenses and threats. This indicates the reason why a client needs a service provider in any case. Let's take an example of any web hosting organization. And, I'm a regular client of this organization that hosts all of my website data, so my own company pays monthly free to this web-hosting organization for facilitating terabytes of website data and traffic for us. In return for that service, we pay them. So, as the service provider, they must deal with all the expenses as well as threats, viruses, backups, etc. related to that service. For instance, we made a fixed fee contract with this organization for the unlimited storage of our data on their web servers along with unlimited bandwidth, without paying extra charges for these services. Let's say I am running a multinational company which has a lot of technical staff and IT experts. So, why my company doesn't manage and have our web-servers to host all of our website's data and online traffic? The reason is that we prefer not to manage the expenses and risks of giving that specific service. It simply isn't the business that we run. Rather, we are concerned about our business that runs on the website. We neither want to run these enormous web-servers nor managing the servers repairing, the backups, upsizing and downsizing (according to the online traffic), etc. So, we have taken the services of a web hosting company, and we made a fixed fee contract with our service provider. We deployed our website on their web server and in return, pay the company a fee after every month for using their resources. In simple words, for an agreement with our facilitator, we took those expenses and dangers from us and put all the hosting responsibility on a service provider by paying every month. We aren't responsible for running several web-servers, domain controllers, mail servers, and file servers anymore. This explanation is referring to the actual definition of the term service.

Let's recall the service definition once again. The term service refers to *the methods of enabling co-created value to facilitate the client's desired results, with the security that the client wouldn't have to deal with the expenses and threats*. Along with the services, a service organization is the one that can deliver services dependent on items they sell. Now, let's take a look at the definition of a product. *A product (item) is the formation of an organization's assets, which is made to give value to the customer*. In simple words, it is a group of services that we set up together to give more worth than they could separately. Every enterprise uses a lot of resources. Now, the enterprises either possess the resources or manage them. These resources can also be supporting services offered by the enterprise's service providers and their business partners. These resources or assets can be rented. These assets could be the individuals who are employees of the company who work for it under some sort of contract; therefore, these individuals are an asset to the association. The essential part of a product is how a company organizes each of those assets into a set offering. How about we take the example of world-leading cloud computing service provider AWS (Amazon Web Services). The AWS has a variety of services such as EC2 brand for web-server hosting, S3 & EBS for data storage, Route 53 for domain name server frameworks, and others as well. These are generally individual services but aren't viewed as products. Now, let's compare these separable services with another AWS product known as Amazon Light sail.

You can perceive how Amazon has consolidated its EC2, their S3, and their Route53 services into a single item that a client can buy it directly. This world-leading service provider eliminated a great deal of the complications and uncertainty related to the adventure of a new client into cloud computing. Thus, we covered a lot of major concepts in this part of the book. I hope that you have completely understood the key concepts and the examples I have discussed earlier in detail. Still, there are two important definitions that you must remember from the exam perspective. The first one is the definition of service, and the second important definition is the product. I don't need to write both definitions, again, and again, you can simply scroll up the document and memorize them. Remember, understanding and recalling the important definitions can help you a lot in the certification exam.

Service Offerings

I would like to quickly discuss the idea of a service offering in this chapter. The reason I spent this lesson on service offerings is that it is a term that you need to be able to address and explain on the test. This definition comes within the comprehend level for the certification test. So the term ***service offering refers to a classification of one or more products aimed at addressing the requirements of a target client group.*** Primarily, a service provider may deliver their products and services in the form of service offerings to clients and users, defining one or more of their services based on one or more of their goods. So, as part of that service offering, it may also include products, access to a variety of resources, and service behavior. Now let us consider an example to explain the concept of service offers briefly. Let's suppose I own a company that provides services to students, preparing for ITIL 4 certification exam. And you are the one studying for this particular exam. So, when you study for your tests, we have several various products that can assist you in exam preparation. Suppose that every lesson includes a series of videos, one or two practice tests, and some access to the professor to ask questions.

Now, in this case, every lesson is a product, i.e., a series of videos or practice tests are products, whereas access to the professor is considered a service. So, when you look at all of this, you might be watching a video as part of a single service offering you paid off. You can watch it as part of a subscription service where you pay for video access like ours every month. It's a possibility that it can be a single lesson that you've paid for. Sometimes it depends on how you access it. Depending on where you got your desired lesson, you probably got a different service offering. Let's say my company doesn't offer one-time sales on our website that offer you unlimited access for a lifetime. Rather than, we provide a membership-based service that allows participants to join each certification lesson we provide at a low monthly charge. That's why we created our video lessons and some practice test classes. As part of that particular service package, students can get many practice test questions before attempting the actual exam.

Consider that my company offers these lessons on other platforms, and they may not offer a membership-based fee service, where, for as long as you want, you can have as much as you like. Alternatively, the lesson may be treated as a single item to be sold. You'll get all the videos, the reference manual, and perhaps one or two practice quizzes for a one-time payment. But if you need more practice tests for your preparation, they'll treat it as a whole lesson, and you'll have to pay an extra fee to get all those practice tests. I hope you have started to get the picture of what a service offering is, as I'm talking about it. This tells you that we can combine and market multiple times these various products and services, based on the buyer we are trying to reach. You might have seen it with many organizations offering products as a monthly service, where various service offerings occur at various prices based on the different features. For example, many people use Netflix at their homes, which is a video streaming service. It has several various levels of pricing. It provides three media streaming options: basic, standard, and premium beginning at $8.99 a month and ending at $15.99 a month, supplying you with all the Television shows you want to watch. Let's say I use the basic media streaming option at $8.99 a month, which permits only one monitor to be downloaded to one phone or tablet at a time in standard definition. So, I have decided to choose another pricing plan, i.e., standard one, which will allow me to pay $12.99 a month along with the advantage of watching two high definition screens at a time. As I told you earlier, Netflix has even a third level pricing, known as a premium package. This subscription package allows you to watch videos at once on four screens (perfect for families) in HD for $15.99 a month.

So as you stepped up the price scale, as part of that service offering, you received extra services. Finally, let's recall the definition of a service offering one more time. A service offering, if you recall, is a classification of one or more products aimed at addressing the requirements of a target client group. Now keep in mind, as part of that service offering, it can also include products, access to a variety of resources, and service behavior. So we're going to describe these three elements before we finish this chapter. First, we've got products (goods). Goods are items that the customer is provided with. These items are passed from the supplier to the customer, and then the customer bears responsibility for this potential use once this happens. For instance, they will give you a phone that you could use if you went and subscribed to a new service offered by your local telephone provider. Now you're in charge of that mobile, however. You'll have to pay to buy a new one if you smash it. If you lose it and someone takes it. He/she makes long-distance $500 calls every month, and then you'll get the bill. The products have been passed from the supplier to you, i.e., the cell phone here, and you are now accountable for it as the customer. Offering access to resources is the second thing a company can deliver. This indicates that a customer has access to the resources, or a license under certain agreed conditions is granted. Consider the same example of my imaginary website. Let's say; you can get access to the videos, the practice examinations, practical laboratories, and all the other material we have when you buy a subscription plan from my website. The criteria you agreed to when you signed in, you're provided with a license to use them in such a case. All these services are under the responsibility of the supplier, and the service provider must ensure that you can use them as planned.

This is where things sometimes get a bit complicated for customers. Also, the way the service provider provides its product may not be appealing to you. For example, because we are monthly fee-based service, our site does not authorize videos to be still downloaded. So, you will no longer have access to the videos if you stop paying your monthly subscription fee. Therefore, we don't allow you to install them all on your computer, because one week you could sign up for service, download all the lessons available on the website, and cancel it the following day. This is the reason that we won't give that video's possession to users. We simply give you the right or permission to use it and use it as often as you like, as long as your account remains open. Now, if you do not like these terms, you will have to find another way to buy this lesson or any other lesson that allows you to have the one-time payment where you can get it downloaded and use it as much as you like. But, this is again up to your partnership with your service provider. As a supplier, we monitor resources and provide you access of the product under this contract. The last part that sums up the service offering is service behavior or product behavior. This term refers to an act performed to meet the requirements of a target customer. Consider a case when you create a website; you need a software tool for this purpose. Now that you have bought specific software, it means that you have a license for using its features. For instance, our company uses a software package as the basis of our education management system on the website.

We have to pay a one-time fee for the software, and thus, we will be granted the authority to use the features of software permanently whenever we want to, without any annual charges being billed. So, this is in the class of products, right? Well, apart from that, we should not get help and receive any upgrades or blobs for just the one-time fee offer. And if the software includes software updates and blobs, and we want these features, then we have to pay for that portion of the service offering, which is referring to service behavior. We, therefore, decide to pay the company an annual membership fee, and in return, we will have access to their personnel 24 hours a day, every day of week technical support staff, and we can discuss issues with the support team, and we also have access to all safety patches and blobs when they are going to be published. This is the difference between products, access to various resources, and the behavior of services. Items will be sold to the customer, and the user will be given access to the various resources on the terms of services in the contract issued by the service provider. On the other hand, service behavior will take care of things like online technical assistance and customer support fees. That's how you are going to remember the important concepts and definitions for your examination.

Service relationships

It's all about being a service provider, yet an organization needs to be more than just a facility. Just as relationships are complicated and sometimes hard in our love life, similarly relations between organizations and customers can be challenging too. So, what a relationship with service is and why it can be so challenging? Let's dig into the concept of a business relationship. ***A service relationship is a collaboration between a service provider and a service buyer that includes the delivery of services, service usage, and management of service relations.*** This is a concept that is quite simple and clear. Generally, the relationship is created when two groups or companies choose to work together. One of these entities might play the role of the service provider during this partnership, while the other becomes the customer or buyer. Let's take the same example discussed earlier in which I own a company's website providing services to many students, and you are the customer for the learning program we offer. You and I have a service relationship in this case. It can be a lot, a lot more complicated. But here I get a little bit ahead of myself. Let's think about the delivery of services first. What is meant by the provision/delivery of services? Well, service provision is a company's activities to deliver the services. It involves control of assets of the service provider, preparation of the delivery of the product, provision of access to customers ' assets, and the execution of the decided service acts. In addition, these services are supported with the help of service level management. The provision of services may also include the delivery of goods to the customer. Now consider when you are going to purchase your new mobile from the cellular supplier. You go to the shop, and the shopkeeper gives you a good mobile, right? And by providing you a new phone number, he activates your cell phone.

This will set up your new user profile, in this case, your new phone number. Then, they allocate various features to your account, such as voice message, then instant messaging, as well as a data plan and other items. You can walk out of the shop by the time they finish with your new mobile, your new number, and activated cellular service. All of that is your service provider's provision. And you're now going to act like a customer who's starting to do the product utilization. Service utilization involves all of the new cellular telephone operations carried out by an agency, or by an individual, that will enable you to use those new services. Service usage requires matters such as accounting, i.e., the cost of your account each month, and all the other activities that you carry out to use the resources of the supplier, such as to check your e-mail or to make a call on the new phone. Moreover, new service behaviors may be required to be carried out. You might be traveling from one place to another, for example, and you want your internet provider to allow international data roaming on your phone. Again, this is one of the things which can occur in service usage. If the customer does something, it is considered as service usage. Other practices are conducted by both the supplier and the customer in relation to service provisioning and service usage. And if they do these activities together, they try to make value co-creation possible on the basis of the agreement. This is regarded as the service relations management.

The most obvious things are things like making the customer pay their bill on time, so service providers don't cancel their monthly subscription, and they don't turn off the service. Or the service provider may have to check that the network interruption that could happen anytime is appropriately conveyed because there will be a system update next weekend. We call this back and forth communication a service relationship model. This model is related to service relations, which includes service delivery, service usage, and client relations management. This relationship is considered as a complicated part of this subject. So, let's dig into it. The business may be challenging, as I said. And this is why we need to understand the multiple partnerships included in any single service. Let's consider the example of having my own company and business website, and you are my customer. Let me make you clear your mind that this is the example of multiple partnerships in a single service. So, on our website, we provide our learners, both teachers, and students just like you, with online learning services. Now, whenever you watch the videos on our website, which indicates many different business interactions, it has already happened in the background to allow it to happen.

For example, you belong to let's say, organization A. And you want to see a video on my website. But that specific video clip should reach to you to watch it. Yeah, that's because you have a service relationship contract with my company. You are the customer in this partnership, and we are the supplier of services. But we are also dependent on other service providers to do this job. For example, we outsource web-hosting service to a large media streaming provider with multiple cloud servers worldwide to ensure you get the highest quality with the maximum throughput, rather than having our web servers and hosting the content. Now, let's place the media streaming provider in organization Z. Thus, in the partnership between my company and the video streaming business, we are the customer, and the service provider, in this case, is the video streaming provider. But the service we use, the media streaming service providers don't have their web servers. No, they are relying on Google Cloud or Amazon Web Services instead. And it means that Google or Amazon will be the service providers, and the media streaming company is a customer too. Yet, to make it even more difficult, teams are operating on IT systems within the Amazon/Google.

They are the subscribers on my website and learning the same lessons that you're enrolled in right now. And, when they're logging in to my portal to view these videos, they'll be the customers instead, and I'll be the service provider again. You can see how this partnership can become very complicated and confusing. The fact of the matter is that businesses will be acting as both along with a service customer themselves with these four firms that we mentioned in this topic. With all the different relationships we have, I would extend every partnership for every product offering inside my organization because we're a small enterprise. If you're thinking about how complicated it would be for someone like twitter, or Microsoft, or any famous social media platform, it will make your head spin. Therefore, I would like to remind you that your company can be a service provider or a consumer of the service. Or maybe they're both. It all varies depending on the situation and the partnerships involved in the service.

Outcomes

As I addressed the concept of service above, I said that it was the method of enabling co-created value to facilitate the client's desired results, with the security that the client wouldn't have to deal with the expenses and threats. So, in this chapter, we will dive into a single word taken from the definition of service, i.e. the results, if customers intend to set up and control their assets of services instead. Now, let's take an example of what we're talking about here. I have two famous transportation companies operating in my local area. I've got Juno and Via. Now, it doesn't make any difference what you prefer. But I'm more likely to take Juno myself than Via. Now, I love transportation services, particularly when I'm going to the large commercial area for a meeting or event, or when I need to get to my home or something like that from the airport. Now, I've got the desired result as a client. With a decent amount of cost, I want to travel from location X to location Y in the shortest possible time.

For example, I didn't rent a car for the last tour I took to NYC because I just used Juno and Via to get to my hotel from the airport and from my hotel to different places in the city for my work. Now, this helped me to get the desired results, which was travelling from location X to location Y in very little time and with less trouble. Then, I was able to minimize my total cost because I didn't need a rental car, as I used the Juno application. I didn't have to spend $75 a night for parking the car at my place. And for that rental vehicle, I didn't even buy fuel. I didn't have to purchase rental car insurance. Here you get the picture. I was able to get rid of many expenses because, as a client, I paid for the service whenever I used it, and I was capable of achieving the desired result, moving from location X to location Y. So, if we talk about the associated risks, I could also reduce some of the threats. For instance, I usually find parking very difficult in big cities, especially near areas of the city which I must visit for work. And when I used Juno, I could remove the risk of not having a free parking area once I arrived at my destination. Therefore, I simply get out of the car without worrying about the parking.

I also removed the risk of someone robbing or trying to break my rental car and steal my bags when it's parked. All those kinds of issues are gone, and, so it's not a thing to be worried about anymore. Now, it seems you're getting the key concept at this point. The various car-associated risks and different costs can be minimized if someone uses a transportation service. And as a rider, I can take advantage of the service by using this transportation app rather than booking my car whenever I need to go on a business trip. But I now have to equalize it to the other side of the ledger. There are some risks and costs that I expect when I choose to use Juno or Via rather than booking my vehicle. First of all, the service provider imposes costs on me. In addition to the current service cost for getting from X to Y, I also need to keep a mobile phone running the app. And I need to make sure I've got a data package on that cell phone. And I have to ensure I have sufficient battery capacity of my cell phone. All of these events will happen so that I can link the application from my mobile to their web server, and the closest Juno cab driver can connect to my phone so that he will pick me up from my place. When I'm in a big city with high parking ticket fees, the traffic is often heavy, and there is a large number of drivers in the town, so when I need a cab, it's fastest for me to have the Via or Juno. However, in a case, when I am moving towards a remote area, I would like to hire a car because it serves my purpose very efficiently. Due to the reason that it will be less risky for me that I won't find a parking area because the parking in these places is cheaper and we can easily get one. Also, the traffic in remote areas is not an issue because it is outside of the main city.

This is the main idea of considering both the pros and cons so we might come up with the idea to find out what gives us the maximum value. So, in all these case studies, we talked briefly about the results until now. There is also a similar approach called as outputs, significant to understand when you take the test. *An output is a deliverable material or immaterial object, or an item produced through an operation.* Now you need to learn the difference between an output and a result for the test. Services from one or several outputs promote results. So, what is that about? An output might be a document. It might be a phone bill you get at the end of the month for using a particular service. And if you use an email service, then it will be a mail. They are all known as the outputs. These are the material objects that appear as a result of using the service. Now, however, I want to think substantially about this concept. Consider this online lesson. The output is the final content you were currently reading when I wrote this lesson. But, this is only the output; it's not the result. Then, what is the result if the written content isn't?

Well, you're aiming to achieve the perfect quality of material from this manuscript. The result for students like you who want to pass the ITIL 4 test lies in all the content of this book as well as other material available online. After learning all the ITIL 4 related content, if you manage to complete that, then you have obtained the results you and I wanted. This is an important subject that people commonly misunderstand it because outputs are easily measurable, but the results are not. Creating an overview and writing all of the content we're going to study in this book is less than an issue for me. Let's take another example in which someone is running a website on which he uploaded all the ITIL 4 related content and a lot of videos, and he gathered all the information by studying several books and online courses. That person may be already teaching this subject in any university or academy. Or, he has passed the ITIL 4 Foundation test and helping other students in their tests. I just want to say that the person has a lot of knowledge about ITIL 4.

As I have mentioned that the person made a lot of videos, for instance, we could assume that there will be a hundred videos in his lesson. And if he has already shot 50 clips, then he completed 50% of the lesson. And so he made 50% of the consumer product. Now, that is calculating outputs. It does not calculate the results. Does he know that the right proportion is a hundred videos to help students by watching from start to the end and pass the test? If the end result is students passing out the exam, then the right way to measure won't be one hundred videos. Perhaps only 50 videos are needed or perhaps 150 videos. He's starting to figure it out and measure it as he goes along. And as he finds out which content is useful and which isn't, he incorporates and eliminates things to the lesson to ensure that students are capable of passing the test. The output is always a part of the final result, but it's more than mere outputs. So when you learn about the final results, I want you to note that it isn't only the created outputs, but you will also attain it as a result of the operation and this interaction.

Returning to Juno and Via example, the final result, in this case, is that I move from place to place easily and reach on time due to services offered by those enterprises. The purpose of taking this lesson is not that you've been sitting here and watching a hundred clips for a specific amount of time or whatever. But it's focused on you passing the foundation test. And that is the result both students and the coach want to accomplish here. Now, as a fact, results can be more abstract where outputs appear to be real, such as objects that you can reach out and touch like documents and records etc. It also means outputs can be calculated more accurately because they are the consequences of an operation. Therefore, you need to be careful not to calculate only outputs while creating product metrics. You have to think and focus more on how you will evaluate your final results too. Otherwise, you'll find people working on that framework for you and play with you. These people will do many things to make you look like all those outputs are quite high, but you will never produce the desired results you need. So always care about it as you construct the metrics. So make sure you evaluate the end results, not just your performance of outputs.

Costs

We're going to talk about costs in this chapter. ***Cost of something is defined as the amount of money invested in a specific business or resource***. While costs are generally described in terms of finance, it can also be expressed completely non-financially. Let us consider the same example of a person who owns a business company and runs a website and uploaded his many lectures and several videos of the ITIL lessons, but this time the person is me. Thus, if we make a new lesson here, the cost and the number of hours spent creating the lesson are calculated. A standard class such as this could take 500 to 800 hours of effort for all our team members. This is generally described in man-hours or FTE measurements. The term man-hours are also called hours for people because we want to give everyone equal chances here. Whereas, FTE is the abbreviation of full-time equivalent, and it is used to calculate things based on a single employee who works 2,080 hours for the whole year which is calculated as 8 hours per day x 5 working days a week. It is the full-time working hours of one employee. If we want to host all our lessons on a web server, half of an FTE or half of the annual working hours of one person for the whole year may be needed. It specifies the number of employees needed for full-time equivalents for a specific activity.

So, if I want to calculate things from a work hour's point of view, it eventually results in financial cost. Most of my company's members get a payment, and if it requires someone half a year to manage the web servers, which means half their income is related to having and running the web servers up. It will eventually return back to its cost. But if we glance at our records, we'll observe that we give more value to the time things take than the amount of cash spent on them. You can now choose to compare things based on the person-hours, the man-hours, the full-time equivalents, or using real dollars that are invested, depending on your company. Either way, the supplier aims to reduce and minimize costs by offering a service. If a service provider may save your money more than even their service will cost you, you'll be looking to use that service. I know I'd do it.

Let us suppose, my web service provider has different internet speeds enabled that we can select and use in my office here. We might select to pay $70 a month for 200 megabits per second link, or $200 a month for 2000 megabits per second link. Which plan are we going to choose? Okay, in this case, because of all the videos we make, we post a lot of big files. And when we checked the internet speed we were buying; we agreed that it was worth it to pay twice money a month for a 50 time's greater speed because it spares our office staff a lot of time and effort uploading those files. It was an easy choice because spending a little more dollars per month on the high-speed internet service made my workers more efficient, saving us a lot of extra hours of work and that more than paid for the extra costs and labour benefits we could get. If you look at the price, that's the point. If you're trying to outsource a product and charge for its service, you need to ensure that it gives you more value and benefit than it costs you. In our situation, we are offered 150 times more value by investing twice on the internet. And so it certainly was worth it.

Risks

I have already addressed the term risk (dangers) a couple of times in the book. But in this chapter, I decided to dig into it in a bit more detail. The term risk refers to a possible incident that could cause damage, failure, or prevent you from achieving your goals. It is any incident that could affect our ability through our facilities to co-create the value. Generally speaking, when most people seem to think about service management threat, they think about it from the perspective of a new machine installation or a project. Still, the risk is also available in our services. From the supplier's point of view, our objective is to reduce the risk for our clients using our utilities. Risks are closely related to costs in this way. But like cost, our clients will believe that as part of their usage of our services there will be some new risk. Let's recall my example of riding with Juno, where I was a passenger using the app to get trips around NYC. I eliminated the possibility of not having a parking area for a rental car as the company removed my need of having it in the first place.

On the other hand, I now run the risk that if the system crashes; I will not be able to call for a Juno, or what if I'm in a no cellular service area? Or what if the battery of my mobile dies? These are all new risks to my desired result of moving around NYC. Now, as a service customer, I can also participate by taking some mitigation measures to minimize the risk. Or I can carry an extra charger with me. So, as a user, I reduce the risk that I can't call for a Juno when I need the ride because of my dying battery. I may also inform Juno driver that, if I'm outside the town, I might not get enough drivers in a certain area, because I'm finding it hard to use their app in the more remote areas. If my demands and requirements are conveyed more clearly, the service provider can decide if they can better address them.

The company may decide to pay a discount or bonus to their riders who will operate outside the central city in those remote areas. This strategy could boost the number of riders on those roads and getting a cab easier for passengers. It is now up to me as a user to express my requirements clearly to the service provider and to specify the results I want to obtain. I must also ensure that I express any shortcomings or major success indicators I might have for the service. It means I'm placing conditions on that service provider, right? So what do you think? As a client, the service provider can also impose conditions on me. For Juno's case, they need me to have a mobile phone, a reasonable data plan, and the ability to transfer my GPS coordinates to their riders through my phone's location tracking app.

After all, this is a two-way road; we are all co-creating the value and reducing the overall threat. Now, as risk is a possible future incident that could cause damage or make it harder for anyone to accomplish our goals, we might do some things to reduce that danger. So, what are the precautions we can take to reduce the possible risk? There are four things that we can do about risks: risk can be avoided, risk embraced, risk transferred, and risk minimized. Now when we want to avoid risk, we seek to remove it from the system entirely. We can't eradicate the risks of a product because the risk is something embedded in everything that an organization does, to some extent and some level. But we can completely avoid those threats. Let's assume, for example, that you manage a platform that allows readers to read your article. Perhaps you're anxious about the new privacy rules and don't like to worry about keeping all of the information of the article viewers, safely and correctly under the new General Data Protection Regulation requirements. Thus, if you turn off monitoring information about your reader by deactivating any cookies, you could easily avoid these problems.

And you also remove any requests for their email addresses and other things like that. If you're not collecting their information, you no longer have to protect that information. Now, this may not be the best business decision. Because most businesses want to be able to track their customers and contact them by email with offers, so while you can avoid this whole situation, it's probably better if we found a better way to handle this risk. And that brings us to accept the risk. And you also delete any queries for their emails, as well as other such items. You no longer need to protect that information if you are not gathering their details. This might not be the best decision for the company, correct? Because most enterprises want their customers to be tracked and contacted via E-mail addresses for new offers, it is better for us to find another way of dealing with this risk, while avoiding the entire situation. And that just takes us to understand and accept the risk.

You look at the cost of securing from threats with this strategy, and you look at potential odd results and consider that it's actually cheaper to pay to take the risk and paying up for it when you are captured. Returning to our example of privacy rules, I have a client who is in a company based in Canada, outside the European Union. Because of this, he's taken the approach that he doesn't care about compliance with the GDPR rules because he is a Canadian living in Canada and he's got a Canadian business. He's not specifically targeting European clients, but he's measured the risk if they choose to go to his website, so he thinks the risk is minimal that the EU will try and find him or even catch him if they do. He has, therefore, made no moves to change the way his company runs or the way his business operates. He will do it exactly as he did before GDPR, as he did after GDPR. This is known as risk tolerance or acceptance. The next action we could take is that we can now choose to pass the risks. You may not want to be accountable for all this private data gathering and handling, but you still want access to that information.

In such case, you will be interested in hiring a service provider to collect, save and access the personal data for you. This is a form of transferring risk. Another alternative might be that you pursue the path my Canadian friend has taken, and if you are sued or charged, he will simply have to pay insurance. It passes the responsibility of risk on to the insurance company, as you paid to pay it an insurance fee to take on this risk for you every month. Our last risk solution is what is used most frequently. It refers to mitigating risks. By incorporating risk mitigation, we can take measures to minimize the risk even if it does not eradicate it entirely. Let's recall the privacy data example in which we can access and manage the reader's personal information if we want to. So, in this case, we can add new applications of technologies in our system to protect the data integrity and to implement new procedures as we manage the data. It can help us mitigate the danger and will eventually secure it for viewers, which is also one of the GDPR's desired results. However, a hacker can still enter into our system and rob all customer information. In this case, we may have lowered the risk, but we have not eliminated it completely. This is the concept of mitigating risks.

Utility and Warranty

Every student of ITIL simply needs to understand the concepts of these two terms: utility and warranty. During your training and in the real world, you will see these terms over and over again. ***The utility refers to the usability of a specific product and service to satisfy a specific requirement.*** That is what the company's product or service actually does. The utility is what we call fit for a reason. Okay, let's look at the warranty for a while, then we'll compare and contrast these two terms, as differentiating these phrases is something you might see on the test of ITIL. ***Warranty is the guarantee of a product or service that can satisfy the specifications agreed upon.*** It's the way the service works. Warranty is about the willingness of the company to do what it has to do. This is often labelled as made for usage. Now, let's take the example of an automobile to compare and contrast these two terminologies. You are a client who demands to drive a car from location X to location Y, and you need to reach fuel consumption of minimum 40 miles per gallon. So you reside in a place where the weather in the summer gets really warm and gets really cold in the winter; therefore, you want a nice, cool air conditioner and a really good, warm heating system. Now let's consider these conditions and decide whether they meet our utility level.

Note, the utility is about something fit for a reason, and if I have a family of four, I can accommodate my spouse and two kids in a four-door car like a Ford Focus model. So, the Ford Focus would be "fit for a reason" to carry my family from location X to location Y, and it would fulfil my utility operations. Besides that, if I purchase a brand new Ford Focus, it will surely have sufficient fuel consumption and a nice AC and a heater. Thus, it will also fulfil my warranty standards. Remember, the made for usage rule is for warranty. Does it satisfy the customer's specified requirements? So since I'm the user, I'm will say it had a gallon of fuel consumption at least 40 miles away along with a working heating system and air conditioner. And the new Ford Focus is sure to meet those needs. This means that it is considered as made for usage. Now, let's say I purchased the car for a couple of years, and my wife's got another child. We've already got two children, so this little Ford Focus won't be very good anymore to carry my whole family around. It won't be for a reason anymore, because whenever I go out for dinner as a family, we'll have to bring two cars now, as we all probably won't fit into the Ford Focus.

The warranty may exist there because the air conditioning unit and heating system are still working, and it still generates 40 miles per gallon. But it is simply not possible to achieve the expected purpose of getting us all from location X to location Y. There are insufficient seats and limited seat belts. And because the utility is about fit for a reason, this Ford Focus no longer meets my requirements for utility. I hope you will understand the difference between utility and warranty in this small example. Note that what service will do is a utility which is riding from location X to location Y. And it must be perceived as part of the warranty that how the service will do it. This gets 40 miles per gallon and keeps the car's temperature normal. It shouldn't too warm or too cool.

Another key thing to remember now is that both utility and warranty are necessary for any service to run effectively. We mostly see people focusing on the warranty in the IT industry, and they just underestimate the utility. If I have a service running on a magnificent, scalable cloud technology that can concurrently support millions of customers, this is a warranty. IT folks like warranty, because the measurement is easy. You have a good warranty if you need a product to have a specified and agreed condition and you satisfy certain conditions. Guarantee simply requires a product to help in the user's performance and eliminate the user's constraints. When, on the other hand, users can efficiently use the product/service to share their latest post online that will be known as a utility.

If the service is always up to date, it does have a good warranty, but it does not operate the service which the user wants it to do, which means that the utility of the service is not good, the service will simply fail. If both the utility and the warranty are not present in the service, you can't run a successful product. Let me give you a few suggestions for the test. A dead indicator of guarantee is if you start discussing issues such as availability, power, security and continuity. These measurements of the infrastructure apply almost entirely on how service does and make it suitable for use. These are, indeed, warranties. On the opposite, when you talk about how it works and does it help anyone to obtain any result, you usually speak of utility which is fit for a reason. Again go back to the example of a car, could it move from location X to location Y? This is called utility. How many miles it gets per gallon and how long the engine will stay up and how cold it will get. All of these are warranties.

Dimensions of service management
Major dimensions of service management

We will be addressing the four aspects of service management in this part of the book. So as we do, this will contribute to the description of four dimensions of the IT service management from the exam's perspective. This is called a two-goal stage Blooms, which means we'll have to explain these four aspects in detail. Obviously, we won't memorize the definitions, but we have to learn how this approach works and how it fits the Information Technology Infrastructure Library. Now, as we speak about the four aspects of

IT service management, we are really speaking about four different viewpoints. So if I have the quality in the centre that I want to co-create, I do it using multiple goods and services that I sell to my client or my buyers as a service provider. Now the end-user and the client has this product, which they are interested in, to get the desired value and that means I need to supply it to them. Therefore, I think about it from four different angles when I go to produce a product or resource, and we name these four viewpoints as the four aspects of IT service management. The first one is people and organizations. The second dimension includes information and technology. The third is suppliers and distributors, and the last one is value streams and procedures, and on the other hand, I have these external factors all around it, which will affect the products and services we make. Now, in this entire chapter, we will talk about each of these four aspects and the external factors.

Organizations and people

Now, this is the first dimension that we will take into account. Although we have mentioned those as one, two, three, and four for the purposes of ITIL, they are not generally in a given order of thought. They're only mentioned this way so we may have a way of presenting it to you within this book. So I really believe that we should talk about organizations and people in the first place as it is one of the toughest to get right. When we're learning about organizations and people in the context of service management, we're concerned about how we're going to build the governance structures to help the services and products we bring to our users, who are those buyers and clients. When we speak about these structured organizations, it could be something as big or macro as the way we establish our company. Will our corporate business be sole ownership? Will it be a limited liability company? Will it be a multinational organization? Will it base in the U.S., or will it be premised outside of the United States?

All these elements are standardized systems of organizations. We arrange the corporate hierarchy within any company or large enterprise. Will we have a very lateral company or very diagonal organization? Let me show you a few examples of that. We're pretty flat in terms of hierarchy. And that means we can directly talk to each other since we are small. We don't need to go upward across networks of bureaucracy. However, in some places that I had previously worked, they had hundreds of thousands of workers. I simply can't go and talk openly to the Director, like somebody in IT. This is simply not how it works. I will negotiate it with my boss, and my boss would speak to his supervisor, then finally, the managing director might get my message. This is an organization very perpendicular, or you may call it vertical. So, when you plan on how to arrange your business, these are things you need to keep in mind and follow them. If you're going very smooth and diagonal, it means you can do things faster, sooner and more productively. The term diagonal represents the horizontal structure, and lateral or perpendicular means refers to the vertical organization. But you need to be much more procedure-oriented in case of a vertical structure. And so these types of queries occur when you start thinking about how will we deliver our items and products through an organizational structure that is highly formal? Also, how will you split up the business if you think in terms of organizations? Are you willing to split your business into marketing and advertising for one department, then into IT infrastructure as another, and then into the support centre for the next unit and admin department in the end? Well, it all depends, and it will all come back down to the hierarchical structure of the organization.

After that, you have to find and work with people when you are done figuring out what that framework is? We need to find the right person to do the right work. This is the essential recruitment and expertise. It is part of all of those human resources. We will, therefore, have to bring the right managers and senior leaders in these kinds of departments after finding out that we have this association and we have all of the separate departments that we have established. And we would hire all the right staff for those departments. And then we have to ensure that these employees keep their skills up to date. I have served in Information Technology for a long period of time. It had been 15 years or more. And machines are totally different now, and our way of running computers was different than we did 15 years ago. Throughout the process, my supervisors and my management had to make sure that I was learning new skills and knowledge so that my abilities and expertise remained with the latest technologies in today's world. Then we must understand each person's duties and responsibilities. What is the role of each individual in this business? What will they do? If you are the all in one person, and you sometimes need to be everything in small companies, where you've got anyone who's going to be the professor, writer or salesman, right? This is the concept of responsibilities and duties. I've got some people who always come and say to me that they want to get into the IT industry or they want to be an IT professional. I ask them what they would like to become in IT because dozens of different job opportunities are available in the IT field. You should understand the objective and the job role you want to accomplish so that we can find out the proper way to get you there.

It takes us to our fourth strong emphasis on organizations and people. And we're calling this a culture. As we speak of culture, we are reflecting the company's shared beliefs and values. And it's the toughest thing to do exactly right. So when you see a new business in the tech industry, most companies start-up, they have a very welcoming environment. It is very casual. You're able to get to the company's manager and say like, "Hey Bernard. How does it go?" However, if you work for someone like Amazon, that's a huge company which depends on procedures and policies, and everything takes place in a very formal manner. So, that's a different environment. Looking at FaceBook or looking at IBM, and then looking at a hospital example, they're supposed to have three diverse cultures. Now, which one of these companies are rights and which are wrong ones? It all depends on how a company manage it so that it can look after the association and the people working for it. Now communication is another part of the tradition, so can we do it individually or by mails? These are all the things within the company that are considered as a cultural thing. How high are the company's honesty and openness? What does your manager say about the organization's intentions? They're sharing the vision or not? Are they sharing aims and goals? All this begins at the highest rank and then goes down. When you're terrible at top culture, you'll have a bad lower culture. So we have to make sure we get our people with the right culture.

At last, when we talk about representatives, we want people who have a sight where they would like to be and people who are committed to the principles and purpose of the organization. So when we say that, the main thing for us is to ensure that we take care of our employees as a family, but then you send them away from the company whenever your people have issues and throw them out, who don't live up to the principles that you set down. And, when you think of these problems, you need to make sure whether this culture works together or not.

These pieces are all when you think about the whole organization. Then we've got its other side, which is the individual man. Every person in a company also has a lot of things, right? Every person has his or her style of management. Your Chief executive might have a vision, and perhaps the same vision or a style of management is different to your first level manager. And that will be a problem. And so when we begin speaking about organizations and people, we need to keep these things in mind. We must also take care of the people in our organization, and update their skills and talents as I spoke before. How do we interact and work with our team members and outside our community? How will we share our technical understanding and share all our expertise? Then we want to focus on how we can promote the creation of value and profit because it's all about tradition, organizations and individuals at the end of the day to do something meaningful and productive. Therefore, to create the product and to build such a service that provides the customer value. We will not be in business for a long time if we are unable to create value to our customers. And that's why we need to consider it. As we conceive about services and products, the first aspect from which we look is through the perspective of the organization and the employees. How we will build up the organization, how it will operate, what kind of cultural heritage it will have, and how we will take care of employees so they can produce and offer those products and services.

Information and Technology

We have the information, and we have the technology in which we will keep the information. It is the viewpoint that we refer to these two separate things. When we discuss the technology, all these things will be dealt with by an information technology professional regularly. These were the computers, databases, cell phones, the laptops, routers, switches, etc. but it's really divided into two different subjects when we think about technology. The IT infrastructure will be supported by advanced technologies, and they will also assist the IT service management. There's a clear distinction as you notice. Now I'm thinking about the IT facilities, and you're Juno, let's say. You provide a transportation service. So which types of technology do you need to deliver service? If you have to send the right rider to the exact location, you need data centres and infrastructure, and you could use cloud technology and cognitive computing, or you can even use the blockchain if you take cryptocurrency for a transaction. All this is the stuff we must do to get your customer with that service.

On the other hand, we have the equipment to help manage services, and when it comes to technology that supports the management of IT services, we talk about things that enable the company to do its job. These things are like managing the workflow. It could be your resources for customer support. It could be interactive cooperation to log in and customize these IT services, certain servers and cloud services. It may also include the service provided to the end-users with items such as mobile applications or stock management systems, but these are items business needs anyway. Let's say you may have an IT service management technology, for example, an Intranet SharePoint channel that serves you based on knowledge. So, it wouldn't be an IT services technology rather an IT service management tool. Certain technologies will be identical. You could use human intelligence in each of these areas, assisting end-users of IT facilities and then supporting the end-users of IT service management technology. In both areas, you can use these things. So this is the part of technology.

Let's now talk about our goods and services for the information side. It is certainly the main direction to achieve this consumer value. You supply information, so supervision of this information is vital. And you provide the service of data mining, so its outcomes as information are very important for you in this case. Management of information has many different risks, but all those various things need to be done so that information can reach the point where it keeps adding customer value. These are things like guaranteeing that information is available, and that information is accessible. The information must be accurate and precise and must be applied. All these are different aspects from which we analyze information; therefore, we are going to potentially have some valuable information if all these six aspects are available. Is new technology compatible? Does it create any sort of budgetary issues, legislative, compliance or information privacy management issues? If I decide to hold more private information of customers, how can I secure it, for example, since laws and regulations require me to secure it? Next, will this remain usable in the near future?

Will it be perfect for the next four to five years if I spend a great deal of money to switch to this new server? Or is it useful for just six months? We want to reconsider if it's not perfect for the near future. If we think about technological advances, will it correspond with the supplier or the customer strategy? Considering the example of our website and online lessons, we just got a plan of where should we go. And which kind of lessons we want to teach, although I may be able to take 40 or 80 different lessons, our portfolio will contain only about 15 or 20 lessons, which is why we correspond with our strategy where some other things don't. You must know what is in alignment with your plan and what isn't when you consider this from your business. If you run a tech company, you may need to have things that develop computer systems; you do not want to start medical services in this company. It's not the product alignment. Next, we will talk about does the company has the right number of skilled people to help and preserve its technologies? Let's say; I want to shift my servers to the cloud, so do I have professionals in my company who know how to operate at Azure and AWS, because I will need their skills, and running cloud database server is different from running our servers.

The next step we have to consider is that in the future, will it have sufficient automation skills and function with fewer people? Because we always try to keep the workload to a minimum scale. We certainly like to automate something that can be automated. Another thing we would like to know is: does it have extra functionality for other goods and services that we can use? This is a decent example because when you think about it, that's how AWS actually began its journey of cloud computing. In order to sell more products, Amazon had to begin setting up huge data centres, but since they did so, they developed the endless amount of competency, and they mastered it, other companies would like to get this ability as well. Perhaps that could also apply to my company. I am going to buy anything for one competency as I am doing another kind of new competency. Still, it gives me other competencies, and that can now apply to my list of goods or services, just as Amazon did for AWS. So eventually, if I move everything to the cloud, how will that work out of a strategy to prevent data loss?

If we consider taking a risk, it will return to our corporation's culture. For illustration, let us consider, when I have a small business in an IT industry, I definitely might not like to take a lot of risks according to the complexity of my company's business and the community I have. These things are things I will take into consideration what advancements I just made. Should I get the cutting-edge that is riskier, or should I consider something more secure, tried and tested? Possibilities to talk about but the fact of the matter for this examination is that we use information and technology to develop our services and goods and find out how this information technology can affect the business in the long term.

Partners and suppliers

Our third dimension is partners and suppliers. Partners and vendors are the companies and the people, but they won't fit into one single aspect. The reason is that we are deeply oriented as we think about organizations and people. We are going to discuss our company and our organization and the people who support it. We will talk about partners and vendors in this lesson. First, let's look at it: the supplier and the consumer of service are here now and have that relationship. In chapter two, we have already brought this up. So, people consume a product or service when we think about this, and there's someone who offers it. We can be the supplier of the service in our organization and sell products to our clients or our service users, right? However, we probably accept offers and services as well, and in that situation, we are the customer, and someone else is our supplier of services. It could be our collaborator; partner or it could be our distributor. It will now rely on your organization's approach, whether you are using a supplier or a manufacturer.

Do you think it's something that is important for our company's business? And if so, it is definitely more appropriate f you take it as a partnership. If it is something not so serious, it can be in the relationship of the supplier. Let me give you an example: my organization works in partnership with organization A and organization B. Thus, organization A is the one who will evaluate you for an ITIL 4 assessment and organization B is the one who writes the examination and all the books. Due to our relationship with these organizations, we have accessibility to resources for a whole year before they are available to readers. This provides us with a lot of time to get it, read it, understand it all and then create all the practice exams and the lessons. We are ahead of time with all the targets. Organization A and B deliver all these things as part of our relationship and, as we link ourselves to them in this collaboration, we provide and contribute to all these important business functions to them, and they receive input from us. You may call it a relationship or collaboration. On the other hand, when I consider the case of the supplier relationship, let's say my company has a bunch of photocopiers in our office.

Now, if you need to have a printer paper or printer ink and toner, that's what we call a supplier. I will go up on Amazon, I will buy several things, it will deliver them to our office, and we will have paper, toner and clips, etc. for the organization. It doesn't matter to me what Amazon will do over the next few months to ensure the supply order continues since I can grab someone else for it when Amazon stops providing the printing resources. This is a commodity. However, if Organization B wants to shut down and no longer offer the certification, then it is very important to our business, and we need to think about it. This is the distinction between this partner relationship and a relationship with the supplier. You've got a lot more purchase in with a partner. You've got communication in two directions. You could display schedules and roadmaps. For example, when the next section of certification comes out, Organization B will already tell us. The first level is the foundation exam, and then more other exams require you to earn a master's degree certification.

We know the roadmap already and when these exams will happen so that all these products can be built into this partnership. I don't care if a supplier like Amazon will alter the paper type they will be delivering next month unless its size is eight and a half by eleven and is white, and a printer prints it, that's okay for me. Yeah, when it comes to collaborations with a supplier as compared to a partnership, it makes a big difference. Now, your vendor strategy will be affected. You could have a lot of multiple vendors. I served in a very large company with thousands of vendors because we had a hundred thousand workers. So, we wouldn't have to negotiate personally with all these people. We appointed a third party called a service integrator instead, and it was their responsibility to handle all of those service providers for us. And so we would pay the integrationist and make sure that they reach out and handle the relationships with all these various organizations, and also ensure that we now have the products and the deliveries we required.

So these network integrators can be beneficial if you are integrating into a range of different services and a variety of different providers. To sum up the dimension of partnerships and suppliers, you're going to work together with your partners to achieve the desired outcomes you want, and where you hold common objectives and risks with the partner and make sure you are together in this business. We are all in it together, for example, Organization A and Organization B and my company are working together. If Organization B doesn't sell exams because its brand falls, then workers don't want to have certification, and that also offends my business. We all must be in it to ensure that the product remains good, that workers want it and that the certification remains important.

On the other hand, if we start talking about vendors, we take it as products and services. This can be achieved by way of formal contracts. The division of roles is clearly defined. Let's say I'm paying z dollar amount and I'm getting z bandwidth. Or I get z quantity of cloud hosting or z quantity of papers. No matter what those things are, it's all managed and deliverable by contracts.

If you do that amount of work, I'll pay you for it. When you export a product, it is viewed as a supplier and not a partnership. Now, all the services and companies may have partnerships or acting as suppliers, will depend on other companies to a certain degree. You can't do anything without other partners around here. There's always someone who is doing these things. For example, you may have a Windows service that offers you Microsoft

Office when you pay the fee. You can pay a membership fee to your Internet supplier for using internet bandwidth for your businesses every month. There's a part of partners and vendors, and all these things are about management and integration of services. The service incorporation and governance requires the use of specially designed integrators in order to achieve optimal coordination of service relationships. What does this definition mean now? Okay, there are plenty of different elements here if you put your focus on it. For example, when I examine my website, I see that my website needs a programmer to write a code for it.

I need a graphic designer to add graphics on my site. I require someone who hosts my website on a web server. I've hosted the recordings of lessons on another web server. So I need someone who handles the credit card processing. We have five or six different service providers involved to operate a basic e-commerce website. I'll get more suppliers if I decided to list them all. Well, we can integrate the service within the company, which means that I can work with all these suppliers individually and ensure that the product is working correctly.

I can also outsource that to a service integration manager. And if I appoint service integrators to do all that for me on a contract basis, they will go out to all those suppliers, get all that stuff, ensure the product's efficiency and then send me back the desired results. If so, they will become service suppliers for me to do service integration, and I will be the customer using their services that I have just purchased. Can you use the services of a service integrator? Well, that varies depending on the strategy of your company. Your approach will be focused on your priorities, your community and your work environment when it relates to vendors and partners and integrators. A lot of other things are happening, and it would help you out in finding what the strategy of your vendor is. However, you just have to focus on the vendors and partners for the test. Partners are closer to us in our business, vendors appear to be more merchandized, and if you are able to hold this clear, you will give a good exam.

Value streams and processes

Value streams and processes comprise the final dimension of service management. Quality flows and processes must identify operations, workflows, controls and methods necessary to accomplish the agreed goals. These are things such as the organization's operations, the way their activities are planned and the efficient and effective manner in which value creation is ensured for all shareholders. Now let's keep this in mind and continue with value flow. A value stream is a step by step process conducted by an organization to create and deliver goods and services to its customers. This will incorporate all the value chain operations of the company. And we will spend plenty of time discussing processes in the value chain. We actually have a whole chapter on it. Allow me to give you a quality stream illustration. A quality flow will have a number of steps. Allow me to show you three steps. I want to go to dinner today so that I will go to a restaurant by car. I'll go inside and walk up to the counter, and I'll order the cheeseburger and fries. This is the first step, the cycle of ordering or order process.

And I get to step two where I will wait for my meal to cook. And then step three, they will give me that food, and I can eat it. It is a value where we will switch from the raw resources, take orders, make the food, and then return the burger to the customer so that he can have his meal. This is a three-step quality flow. There are some processes in it, such as frying the cheeseburger, adding the ketchup and the sauce, and then bringing it to me at my table. All of this is value-added. This brings me worth, and so I pay for it. However, certain elements are not adding value. For instance, if the fries are cooked, the oil is wasted. In fact, this is perceived as waste. You will throw it in the trash and pay to take care of it. This is an event that adds no value.

There are also activities, such as they have to throw away this wrapping of all the cheeseburgers. It is also a waste. I leave my cheeseburger and create a mess when I'm leaving the table. This is an unnecessary operation without value for the company. And they will waste time and money cleaning up this mess. Some activities bring value and waste in everything we do. And we always aim to reduce the waste in businesses so to increase the value. So, that was an example of value flow processes. We apply these three steps in almost every business. We will take the order of product or service, we will make it, and we will deliver it. And these are events that add value. However, there are also some waste processes along with the added value.

We want to maximize the value flow so that we can reduce the number of activities that are not value-added while increasing the amount of value-added events. After we do it and make it right, then we want the process to be as automated as possible. Let's get back to the example of cheese hamburgers for dinner. Well, if you recently went to a Burger King, you would have noticed that they moved to automation. The orders-taking procedure is removed and the cashiers eliminated. They have these huge tablets placed in the shop, and then you go there, order your food, and pay by credit or debit card. It erased what they thought was an unnecessary added event of non-value, i.e. taking your order from a cashier. Now they work on you as a customer and focus on preparing and delivering the tasty food to you. This is the principle of enhancement and automation here. Now, what exactly is a process when we look at them? So, it is just a series of interconnected or interacting events, which converts some input into an outcome.

We have created processes for a special purpose. We had a value flow in my previous example that consisted of one process with three different events. The process involves the activities of placing an order, the production and the delivery, and we have reached a certain goal. Our objective was to get Peter his dinner. And this is what we call the concept of process. Give an input, a certain number of activities take place then get a result. If you identify your processes properly, you can increase your production efficiency and can also maximize it, so that the automation gets accomplish effectively. And therefore, in this dimension, we have gathered both of our value flows and processes. We will ask ourselves a few questions while looking at our services and products. We'll say: "What is the standard service delivery method of this company?" What steps do we have to take to make this service work? What are the processes, mainly? And which set of procedures give us the right value flow when we placed them together? What are the quality streams that will help deliver the negotiated service outputs? Let's recall the example of me running a website and hosting my lessons videos on it. There's a variety of things that can happen if I think about giving learners the delivery of this lesson's videos. And I divide them into value flows, and each of these parts, each step, is the process inside of it. We need to think about what and how each service action is going to be done. Once, break it down into the different procedures so that we can grasp it. This is why our fourth element is called value flows and processes. If we look at this, we find out how we can send customers this product or service through specific processes as part of value flow.

Service Value System

The service value system will be explained briefly in this section of the book. It is now related to one of the exam's objectives, namely to define the value system of services. For this examination perspective, you will also make sure that you fully comprehend the service value system and its components. Let's begin with what's the term SVS mean? Well, it describes how all any company's components and operations team up as a system for the co-creation of values. These components and actions are all connected within the organizational resources and can be flexibly designed and redesigned based on factors in numerous different pairs. In this way, all various operations, procedures and teams within the organization, as well as specific authorities and roles, must be combined and organized through order to make it fully effective. Some companies are far more versatile than other organizations.

Some are tight and stiff in their ways, but you can use this service value system very rigidly and flexibly, depending on your company and its culture. It depends on your company and how you handle it. Now the primary function of the service value system is to assure that the utilization and management of services and goods within the company constantly co-creates value for all the shareholders. Now, it's three basic elements that we'll see when we discuss the SVS model. In this model of ITIL 4, on the left side, you see that we have demand and opportunity, which is our input. We have value on the right side which is our output. And then in the middle, we've got operations and all other stuff which we are going to discuss right now. We have the service value chain in the middle, and we will talk about the service value chain in a whole chapter of this book. You have governance and practices in the service value chain as well; we will learn a great deal about practices in its own section.

It's the last three sections, and then within item four, we will discuss 34 various practices. Then we have leadership or governance, which is how the organization works. We spoke a bit about leadership before, and in this chapter, we'll discuss it again. We have then the guiding principles and constant improvement. However, the guiding principle is vast, so we will spend a whole chapter on it. So I would like to say, welcome to the service value system before we go any further, and in the next lesson, we will begin to work on opportunity and demand and value, these inputs and the outputs.

Opportunity, Demand and Value

In this section, we are going to discuss the inputs and outputs in the form of opportunity, demand and value. If we look at the Service Value System, it will take inputs from demands and opportunities, and it will carry out several processes and activities. Such processes are carried out using guiding principles, the leadership and continuous improvement to get an output in the form of value that we intend to share with our clients and buyers. If we talk about these inputs, the first thing we have is the opportunity. Opportunities provide ways or options to create value for shareholders or strengthen the company.

We will discuss some examples of this here. Let's take the previous example of my website. So now, if we are going to discover new industries or new clients, we must develop a new product or a new service. There are many different ways in which we can find out these possibilities and then market them so that we can contribute to adding value. As a partner, I am not able to sell vouchers to the students when I first started to teach ITIL. And let's say my students went to organization A to buy exam vouchers after they finished my class.

The students would then order their voucher, pay upfront for the exam, and then take the examination. The issue is that they must pay the full market price. Now, one thing we can do is to do a partnership with organization A and B so that we could get those coupons and buy them in large quantities. By doing so, we will get them on a cheaper rate and resell to our students with half of the market price. So now our students can visit our website, purchase these vouchers, and could save about 50 dollars off the actual cost as they buy it from us. It was one way in which we could offer a product to our customers with more value. It's not our service because we are not providing it. Instead, we only purchased the vouchers in bulk, so we will sell them out and pass them on to students. Thus, it adds value to our students because they can now purchase their learning and certification tests at a much lower rate from us. We planned to take this opportunity, and therefore we have built up different procedures and practices so that you can receive your coupons in this way.

Now we will discuss demand as our other input. So demand is when the internal or external customers want or need some of your services and products. So how does demand look like? Well, if you are running a company, you would get it every day. In my case, I've got students who complete an exam, and they tell me in an email that, they passed the test. Then they ask: are you offering this new certification? Or, if you provide this certificate, I'd appreciate that. So they act as a client, and outside customer, who wants and demands a service from our organization. I have already told you about the certification in the first chapter of the book. The ITIL4 Foundation test is the first certification exam, and then there are other high-level certifications. Many students who pass the foundation test, they could ask us if we offer the next certification exam. So, what we can do in such situations? We could provide that course as well to our students who have passed the first one. We can take input from them and work on it, which helps us decide the goods and services we will offer. The students mostly want more of the hands-on experience of our training lessons. So, rather than just watching a video lesson, I can build labs in which students can log in and perform actual actions.

These are the types of things the demand has generated, and we have now created such goods and services that can come from the other side and give our students value, through our service value chain and the SVS. It gives us the results of the service value system, which is its value, i.e. the output. And in this regard, the Service Value Systems will allow a wide range of stakeholders to create many different kinds of value. There is also a value that an organization gets when we talk about value and see it from a service perspective. So when we spoke about the test vouchers, we get a benefit from doing that. When we purchase them all and do all the processing, we keep some money, and we make some profit from it. So my company has value in doing so. We need to pay our workers, and we have to pay more expenses to do so. For our other participants, our students, there is also value in this offer. Students get 50% off rather than paying the full market price.

So, that's helping students save so many dollars and giving them the right thing. There are quality and value we offer you. We could have other organizations ' interest. For example, I would have some contracts with many schools. They will buy these coupons when they go through the ITIL 4 lessons and teach their students. But they don't purchase it for the same price we do, because we buy thousands of such coupons a year. And it's a much less price for us. And so we sell these vouchers for the groups of students of 30 or 40, to these colleges. And they are going to get coupons a little cheaper than a single student because they will be purchasing so many of them. Again, we are valuing the same service or product for a range of different investors here.

This situation can occur in the process and operation of the Service Value System. The enormous server farm was built by Amazon to host its website, and they go so that we could sell it to other firms as well. And they provide services; it's called web services from

Amazon, i.e. AWS. And this means that they can take it and give various shareholders a different value. It is the main idea here. Therefore, we see the Service Value System from left to right, in which we look at possibilities as inputs, new businesses, new clients, new services and new products and what the people want, internally or externally, to purchase. We then see the value for all these internal and external clients, the organization, business, all your users and buyers on the output side. This is the concept of SVS. Bring something in, add value, and get the desired results out from the other side.

Governance

We will discuss the theory of governance quickly in this lesson. And in the service value system, you will see it. It will be part of that internal component that takes our possibilities and our requirements and works around this middle of the SVS to bring out the value on the other side. What's the term governance means, now? It is a way to control and manage an organization. I have used the example previously. When you think of your government, like the United States, congress here, do the governance. They provide for legislation and regulations to be followed by the rest of the industry. Well, you're running leadership within your company. Those in the C-Suite can establish governance. It could be your company's Chairman, CEO, or other senior managers.

You must establish the way the company is directed and managed, and then transfer them to items like rules and regulations and benchmarks through governance. The centre of ITIL is a governance structure, but it is not a governance directive structure. It won't tell you to must follow all that ITIL says it is. Instead, ITIL is a good practice, and you can develop ITIL-based leadership and governance. If we look at the leadership of your company at a broad macro level, this is the way you will be doing everything. You can figure out how you manage things like change management, with the help of procedures and activities.

Whenever you need a new server, there are 15 multiple steps and many different approval processes at that level to undertake this process. This is a governance part. The entire idea of governance is the way how you regulate, organize and run your organization. And, if you talk of governance like regulations, that's the main idea of it in your organization. And it is a component of the service value system, as governance is what you are building up your processes and your activities to ensure that they adhere to what is outlined in the organization's strong governance system.

Guiding Principles

The seven guiding principles of ITIL 4 will be examined in this section of the book. Now that is valuable because two test objectives covering these seven guiding principles are on the examination. First of all, the nature, use and engagement of the seven guidelines should be described. Secondly, the use of these distinct guiding principles should be explained. And it is beneficial because we won't necessarily have to memorize or find out what the guiding principles are. However, we need to describe and classify them, which is a level two effort within the examination. If I provide you with a scenario and describe all of these guiding principles, then you have to be able to select and say, this guiding rule is related to this scenario. We have to talk about what is a guiding principle before we explore deeper about everything. Well, the guiding principle is a recommendation, which in all circumstances guides a company or business.

Guiding principles are used to direct a company in their work by adopting a service management strategy and adapting ITIL guidelines to their own specific needs and conditions. It implies that all enterprises must incorporate the use of multiple approaches to service management into their overall approach. The way you manage services and the way I manage services may differ, but we should both be centred on the same fundamental principles. It is because these governing principles are universally applicable to each program. Such guiding principles will allow us to support and encourage our companies, through their continuous development throughout all stages, as we talked about adopting the guiding principles. As I said, these are universally applicable to all projects, but also all of your various shareholder groups. So, all of these people have to be addressed when you learn about guiding principles as we speak of consumers, buyers and investors in the organization.

The Focus on Value rule is the first guiding principle. It can and must be implemented to all the shareholders and the corresponding value concepts with Focus on Value rule. We will not only acknowledge the consumer's interest, but we also want the customer's interest to be taken into account. We want to look at the value for the supplier. Everything that we do and every service which we offer must bring value from all these different users and shareholders. And so, we look at this thing as we consider the principle of Focus on Value. Now, I will not use only two or three of these principles as an organization. However, I should think of all the seven principles to decide which ones are important and how I should use them for each scenario. Five or six of these principles could be applied to your businesses as all of them will not be critical for you. Then you'll need to go through each one of them like a list, to ensure that you think analytically about your products and services. In doing so and evaluating each one of them, you have a way to decide if they are suitable or not and will apply to your company.

So far, I have listed many of these principles, but I didn't even let you know what they are. Okay, we will concentrate on the seven fundamental principles throughout the rest of this chapter. Focus on Value is the first guiding principle, whereas the second one is Start Where You Are. Progress with Feedback is the third guiding rule. The fourth is the Visibility of Promotion and Collaboration. The fifth is Holistic Thinking and Work. The next principle is to Keep it Simple and Practical, and the last one is to Optimize and Automation. Let's begin with our seven guiding principles.

Focus on value

We are going to discuss Focus on value principle. This principle says that all the companies operations have to relate explicitly or implicitly to its own, clients and shareholders ' value. Now, how can we use this focus on value rule? Now, when I talk about focusing on value, there are four stages in this method which I like to use. First of all, I want to know and recognize the user of services. Who do I try to serve? If you recall the chapter of value, we always use a co-created value between the supplier and user of the service. I can comprehend the service user's perception of value if I find out who that service user is and how they intend to use my service. For example, a student is using my service who wants to watch lesson videos for passing out the ITIL 4 certification exam, and then I need to know how he wants to use it. Will the student plan to use his laptop all day or will he be on a cell phone? And does he have enough mobile data to watch the videos if he is using his mobile device? Or will he download the documentation and all the videos in advance?

These are all things that we must take into account when developing our service and how we can offer our customers the best assistance and value. After that, I try to relate the value to the desired results, and these results will change over time. I used the example of ITIL 4 certification exam many times. You take this lesson so that you can clear the test. Then you can return and read the book (or see the video lectures in the previous example) again after you cleared the test. But now, you do not want to clear the test, and you have a different objective and expected outcome. You did that already. Then, you want to go back and analyze and become smarter in some areas, so you must take this time and use it for your business. That's why we get two different results. One is a group of learners who read the book or look at the videos for the test. The other set of students take the lessons to improve their work and can apply ITIL 4 within their organizations. And that's the fourth step to us. And the last thing I see is to understand the experience of consumers and clients.

Now, that's all about how your client uses your product or service, what they try to do in it, and do you do it in the best possible way? For example, in the case of videos lectures, a mobile app may be made by my company to allow you to use your Android or iPhone for all your videos. That could work well if many of my clients use a mobile device to consume our data. However, if we notice that all of our users use this product by sitting on a computer or a tablet, then it's not worth spending money on creating an Android or iPhone app. Thus, there isn't much value there. This is the idea when we consider these four steps. There are a number of key factors when we look at the app. You would like to know how your clients use every service. Besides, you want to motivate your employees to focus on value because you'll have a variety of people to help your consumers as your company and business grows. That could be technical help. It could be client service providers. It could be sales officers. They could be company managers.

Regardless of what it is, the entire office has to understand what the value is in order to meet the clients' expectations, and then we can make this a leading vision for all employees. We like to do this when we focus on value during organizational activities and enhancement plans. Every day we focus on value over the entire production, whether it works today or to improve it tomorrow for future use. Finally, I need to ensure that every step of any enhancement program must focus on value. I have to find out what parts I should improve if I choose to go back again and rewrite the book. And I'm considering the value for my customers or my students who will get it. If I go back to this chapter, I have to add something new that will improve it and help you better grasp the topics, and allow you to take more advantage of it. I am talking about this idea. All we do is to focus on value for our customers and us as suppliers.

Start where you are

We continue with our second guiding principle. It's a very important principle, as every time you enter into a company, they already have processes and services in place, even when you're a new employee. And if you are active in enhancement programs, you will realize that we don't want to begin each time with a blank canvas and create a new service or procedure to provide a voucher delivery to my clients. Whenever someone comes to this platform to buy an exam coupon, you should see how the process is done. And then, you can figure out what is the better way to do this. But if you don't begin where we are at that moment, and you start off the beginning, you will spend a great deal of time and resources on things we are not doing today. And there is definitely value in the way we are doing it right now.

And therefore, when you are involved in an enhancement plan, I do not suggest you get started unless you first look at what you can use. If you decide how to proceed, you need to consider this based on the precise information gathered by your direct analysis, supported by relevant and efficient measurement. So once again using the same example, if I've brought you in, you will see how we currently achieve our voucher. If you came to us before, you would have noticed that a customer would purchase it on this platform from our shopping cart, which would notify me through email. I ordered the voucher, bought it, sent it via email and forwarded the email to the client. It was a manual procedure. I would then go and buy the voucher, take the voucher, e-mail it and e-mail it back to the student. If you checked it at that time, you might say, I can do this way faster, and I can even simplify it. We can do this task in multiple ways, but if you looked at the way we did it, you would know the right steps to take for this process. We would have to purchase the voucher from other service providers, and then we would give it to our students and receive its payment from our students.

So we must learn about these steps and find out the current steps and the speed of the process and to know the pressure points. You will solve them when you try to go ahead, and some of the pieces from which you start are helpful. Some of them won't be useless to you, and you will push them away. It is achieved by calculating the information and measurements used to help your observations, instead of simply replacing it with nulls and numbers. We focus too much on other aspects in data analytics, and we handle certain basic things we need to look at with our own hands. Our voucher process was very simple if you checked into it, but that continued to work as we started out, because maybe we sold two vouchers a week. We sell lots of vouchers a week now, and if we were to do all this manually, it wouldn't work; it would take a lot of time to send to our students.

We have worked on it with the help of calculations, so we had our time down, now in just five minutes we are delivering a voucher, and a lot is automatic. There are few segments of the process that are still manual, but this is only because these processes run in this way. We're gradually improving it to reduce the time needed to give our consumers greater value and experience. Now the calculating process will affect the outcomes, which is important to think. As you go through all the things that are happening and attempt to measure it, the way you operate can change as you know that they are being measured, this happens very much within the service desk environment.

When you measure how fast a call is resolved, you will see that your first-level operatives will close the trouble tickets. Turning back to the Burger king's example, let's say every customer in the car needs their food within 1 minute, so we don't try to give the customer good quality food any more, but instead, we try to get them in and out within 1 minute. So you have to be careful about that. Thus, measurement is useful for businesses. We use a lot of measurement, but make sure that you calculate the right stuff, and it's not the objective in itself. You evaluate things to decide that the results you really want have accomplished. We spoke about this earlier when we discussed measurement outputs versus measurement results. It is an important idea to keep in mind. So how can we really enforce this guiding principle as we think about continuing where you are? First of all, I want you to think as objectively as you can. You could come to a new location, and they let you in since our current service management model is terrible, you are going to be hired.

When you come in, you would uninstall all they have and start it again. Check out what else is there; find out what is important and what you can draw on. You can decide which good practices or products can be reproduced or improved across the company, and you can also decide to eliminate the flaws and the issues that must be changed or removed. In your decision-making process, you want to add your risk mitigation skills if we eliminate everything and continue from the start. We'll spend extra time and take a lot of chance because something can be repaired way easier than creating something new. You should also understand that sometimes it is impossible to reproduce from the current condition and that you just have to generate a blank canvas. So, whenever you do that, you need to consider the way transformation can be made. Let's take the example of me hosting my own website and sharing video lectures on it. So, my website would be a good example for this concept, when we shoot the video, my website will be updated and improved. And not only is the website itself updated and its feature and graphics, but the entire core services were recreated from scratch.

We had a pair of hundred students in the start, and the existing vendor was good. When we expand, they may no longer meet the demand, and their methods are not working well for our company's long-term goal. Then instead, we design a whole new system from scratch. We've got a brand new OS, completely new databases, a new cloud platform. And the whole application layer is developed, which deliver the lessons itself. It means that we are taking a huge risk because we're moving from something we think operates to something we're trying to operate. Managing risk and reduction are very important, and one of the aspects is when we have split up the phase implementation of moving stuff into pieces. When we first introduced the new website, we did bring the home page, but we dropped the shopping cart, the old content and lessons. Now, we bring parts of the shopping cart, and then we add the big stack, that is our training management program. We do this in very calculated phases over three months.

And when we're through it, most of the old website data won't be reused again, it'll be discarded, as most of it will not apply to the new systems and products we have created. And, sometimes it happens, but I would encourage you to always look at what you can do to reuse the old content for the existing system. In our situation, many of our old lessons could be reused, and our practice tests could be reused, our PDFs and our videos could be transferred to a new website so that we don't need to recreate those lessons again. But many of the services and products underlying the structure are reconstructed from scratch because it cannot be used again. When you begin from where you are, you have to know what things you can recycle when you move through your organizations. So, what should you start with? This is what we are using as our second guiding principle.

Progress and Feedback

Our third guiding principle is progress iteratively and feedback. So, if we operate in a time box iteratively, feedback cycles will be built into the system. This will enable us to be more flexible and to respond much more quickly to our existing client and company needs. In addition, we can identify and react earlier to our flaws and enhance our quality factors. All of this relates to doing things in an agile manner. There are two basic ways in which we can create things when we learn about project management. It can be done by using a method of a waterfall or by working in an agile manner which is more like an agile methodology of Prince2.

Now I have to discover that latest vision with a waterfall, but until everything is done no one can use it. For instance, I would do this if I were planning to build a mansion. I'd find out where the mansion will be built. Before I can give you this mansion, many specific things should happen. I need to ensure that the basement has been dumped, I have to make sure that the walls are up, the power is installed, the plumbing, the drywall, the painting are ready, everything must be prepared, and you can then enter. It may, therefore, take me 15 months or 20 months until the mansion is ready to deliver. Now, if I did these things in an agile manner, I might probably make a room in the mansion first, and you could move into the room and stay in it. Now we can build the rest of the mansion around you and give you a bedroom one by one, two rooms, then three rooms, and then the whole mansion. In a mansion, it doesn't function well, but you can use it very often in IT and services.

So you need to reflect on that when you build service in IT and also on how you can move with responses iteratively. It means that we will divide the work into smaller, more convenient pieces. For example, if I create an android app, once I launch it, it may just have one feature and then the second function is inserted, and then the third function. I could do it sequentially or at the same time. I'm able to make this inconvenient, smaller pieces of code, and then when I make the most out of it, I can hear the audience's suggestions that we need changes in it or we need more of it. And that leaves me with some real results, did I hit the target? Do I have to switch to another thing? It's also great as I get reviews on time. It might only take me almost two months to create if I add a section, and you can tell me, you know that this feature isn't good for me because something else must be added.

Meanwhile, if I've been waiting a whole year, you're staring at it and saying, no! I don't like it, and then I need to work on it for another year. And construct on them in order to improve them in future.

Now, this feedback cycle is important in it because I get reviews from my end users or my investors when I produce such small modular parts. And the feedback cycle is a condition in which part of this output is now a new input operation. Since I give you some code you may therefore say, I like this program, but it does not have a green icon. I want a green button to have it. This will now become an input, which will be returned to the second version with a green icon. Response questionnaires from customer care are a perfect example of this concept. If I run a call centre, after a call, I will receive user feedback I helped, that says how much you were satisfied with us? If you aren't, kindly let us know the reasons, and we will work on them. Then I can use it to incorporate other stuff into the process. Now that we do things iteratively and we do things in those smaller pieces and receive that feedback, we can have those initiatives.

And all the elements break up into these tiny pieces are continually reconsidered to respond to changes in our conditions. Perhaps the demands will change, perhaps the market has changed. The number of day sites was enormous if you visited many years ago. Then everyone would just bring them out quickly and see what happens, but you definitely won't do very well with them if you try to do a deal on the site today. So instead, no one needed that service if you saw that it didn't come onto the market, you would tell me, and what would I use from that?

Now we will have all of these items split into smaller pieces of code like we have discussed before because of our desire to improve iteratively. Those systems, processes and services could be smaller. Now, we will take our program and split it into these different elements, and we shall get feedback across each of these iterations. So, as we collect the feedback, we will start to reconsider our entire code and will cause changes in our next release of our products depending on that feedback. Now that we search for all of the feedback, we have to ensure we don't simply gather it and don't do anything. We want this review to be used in reality. We want to use this before, during and after each of these repeated cycles. This is why, as we tend to use these feedback cycles among all clients, it allows us to understand the origin of the project, where the outputs of this project go, and how this impacts the final customer, and their affected results. We get more feedbacks from knowing all of this, which helps us to work better.

All this has to do things in an agile manner since it's excellent for marketing. Therefore, I want you to progress iteratively by taking help from this lesson and feedbacks, as you move through; you will do things by understanding the whole, but making small pieces towards your goal. So when I talk about building that mansion again, I have to think how will the entire mansion look like, but I'm oriented on constructing one room at the present moment. This is how one bedroom can be built, then the second, then the third room. If you do this in a service or software environment, we create these modules to provide us with the full service. Also remember that, when we think about it, feedback is vital.

When I sell anything in the market, I can hear from my clients that this feature doesn't matter to them, that the service doesn't matter to them, so we need to step forward and do something else. The other thing that I want to remind you is that fast doesn't mean unfinished. Although I give you just one feature or one piece of code, this feature must be finished and it must have the ability to do the entire function it is made for. But then, a second or third function might be introduced to the next version. Version one product was pretty much complete, and there are two features in version two and three features in version three, and you continue to add as you move on. The whole idea here is that we can bring out things more quickly in the market, and we can receive feedback and include them in our future iterations.

Collaborate and Promote

Our fourth guiding principle is known as collaborate and promote visibility. It is all about working with our employees and even our clients as we discuss it. We have a program that contains the right kind of people playing the proper role. We are benefiting immensely from enhanced buy-in, higher value and an increased chance of long-term success. All this requires cooperation and teamwork. We have to exchange data. We have to establish and maintain trust. We have to create understanding. We must realize that when we collaborate throughout the departments and come out of our small compartments, there can be a real achievement. For example, if I build a new product and want to develop it all entirely in the IT sector, but the marketing team will be affected, and it will not work in the long term. When we create this Product for customers, I should instead bring people from the sales department to work and collaborate with us. Since we better acknowledge their roles and expected results. We know how they will operate with this system. Therefore, in working together, we will get a better product, which will also improve visibility in the other aspect of it.

They should realize where we are in the process of developing. It will make them happier and will help them learn precisely where we are, and if we reach our goals, and we will get the product out on time to do what they need. If we look at this, people in all of the shareholder communities are looking forward to the positive collaboration. You don't have the real answer alone, but we can find better ideas if you collaborate with everyone else. The service provider also has to work with its clients. The programmers must cooperate with operations. The distributors will cooperate with the company. All these alliances will provide an excellent result for us. What will happen if there is no accessibility, and there is no good visibility? Well, we start to feel that work is not a primary concern here.

For example, I am creating a website for some marketing department, and they don't necessarily understand that I have 20 other activities to work. They only know about one task, so they will think their task is the most important thing. They may only want a little change on the website. Maybe some font shades they'd like to modify. Does it matter to change fonts rather than fixing something down that costs us money? No, because you don't have contact with them, they don't know about it. I go through it and tell clients that I know it is your priority, but this is not the top priority at the moment because we have more important tasks to do. This is how you must be transparent. You need to show people the location of your outages. Tell them what you work on and show them a view of when you get to your specific problem. If you are not visible enough, your work will lead to bad decisions because someone above you might not comprehend all the things on which you are working.

Your supervisor comes up and says that the marketing manager came in and complains that the font is grey, not black. I want you to change it at this moment. Drop all other tasks right now. He may not even know that you are currently focusing on a server failure that prevents your organization from processing payments for your debit cards. And it costs you, say a hundred thousand dollars per day. This is more crucial than changing the grey to the black font. Therefore, you have to care about this type of thing. Make sure everyone gets to see what the organization works on the side to side. It helps everyone to understand the workflow. The technical problems and the excess capacity that exists can be identified.

And we can eliminate duplication and make sure we all work much better. You might have some kind of a panel while you work in an agile area of growth, which demonstrates what people work on at the moment. What type of work is being done, what work must be done, and what work has been done. It is an ideal way to enhance visibility. The agile strategy I see is what is known as a radiator of data. This is a broad panel in a central area that displays the performance map of already completed work, the threats we have found the problems and other important information. This table shows what we are focusing on. That shows us what you have and what you're operating on. It's completely transparent. It is eternal in cooperation and visibility. I need you to think about that as we talk about the key elements of cooperation and visibility. Collaborating does not mean to imply consent. What do I say by this statement now? I want you to work together when it gets down to it. I need you to work together as a team, but somebody is responsible for the task at the end of the day. Someone is responsible for this service, and that person has the authority of decision making.

They will consider the feedback from all the suggestions they get, but essentially they are the decision-makers. This is why cooperation, communication and visibility are essential because the decision-maker will decide which path to follow and how the service will be created. Next, I would like to remind you that communication is a vital element so that people can hear and understand it. I won't tell them about bits, bytes and all of the technicalities of the service when I'm going to work with the marketing department. Now, we will think about outputs and results. What are they looking to get from this service? What will they bring in and what do they expect to come out? Speak to them so that they will be able to listen and comprehend.

Furthermore, keep in mind that only noticeable parts of the project can be decided. So if you have a lack of good visibility and you are not well aware of your pain, your problems and your risks and don't understand them all, governance can't take the right decisions. It's also part of that cooperation and visibility. Try to ensure that the information reaches to the right people at the right level to make good decisions.

Think and work

Holistically, think and work. This principle states that we must follow a holistic approach to service management, and this ensures that we have a comprehensive view of all the working components together. Take your car, for instance. You sit in your car and drive it, and your output is a dynamic part of your machinery. If you have a holistic view of your car., there are various systems, from engines to braking to AC control that all need to work together to make the machine working. You have to understand it better and how it fits together. Now, as someone who drives a car like me, do I need to know all the components of the vehicle? Of Course not, I just need to learn the holistic approach to it. I can, thus, fully understand its usability by putting the key in the car, turning it and letting it drive me to my destination. We now need to make sure that we consider all four dimensions when looking at our IT services and ITSM because it will ensure that we view it holistically. I would take the information and technology aspect, the value flows and procedures as well as my organization and individuals once again.

I'm going to ensure that I have a clear, holistic approach of how the service works when I use these four aspects of IT Service Management. I will take a strategic approach by looking at the input, the opportunity and demand of Service Value System, as it moves through the centre of the service value chain, along with the leadership and the continuous enhancement and guiding values. And then I can understand everything more holistically with the use of those two frameworks, its four dimensions, and this value-for-service model. I want you to know that infrastructures are complicated, and you need to know that many inputs and outputs are available. So I have to look at everything from a holistic field. Things are seldom as easy as first, second and third steps. In general, steps one, two and three are there, although they are influenced by a number of processes or steps outside themselves. I'll have the website and the software for a web server in case I use something like it. It is, however, an underlying OS, an underlying database, network, it's all connections that are all interconnected.

If I understand how complex a system is, then I'm able to understand its simplicity on the other side of it. I am going to explain it here. We discussed cooperation in the fourth guiding principle, which is an important element of functioning holistically. Cooperation is truly the key to holistically think and work. When I serve in IT, I would be able to understand all bits, bytes, networks and communication. But maybe I don't understand what the bigger company is looking for as an outcome of this service. I have to ensure that when I look at this service, I cooperate with the people who will sell the service and those who will market it. Those people who support the service and if we all consider it from all different angles, then we are able to ensure that we look at it in a holistic and integrated manner. We want to try communication patterns among our various system components, where possible. What are the inputs or outputs of the system that will affect the performance of that system? You must consider all its complexities to make something really simple, and when you know the complexity, you can get it back into a simple representation.

For example, I worked with a company recently, and we tried to gain knowledge of how their network security posture was created. There were so many sub-systems in their network security system that are all worked together to give the company a good network safety posture. We had to move on to people from the various programs running across security stack to understand what the difficulty was and how to reduce it. So we started to improve the program when we did that. The other one has four and five functions. The other program worked four, five and six and each of the interactions between all these various systems would continue to be deeply complex. Then, we can just see as we go back from a holistic security perspective. Again, you need to understand the difficulty of something first if you want to keep things simple. Then you can try to minimize the complexity and ultimately depict it as an efficient solution. Eventually, you may want to use the automation when operating holistically. When we take the example of an incident management process, the service desk will definitely be the point of entry for any accidents that the company reports.

They're your help desk in the first row. They'll sign them, categorize them and label them, but then the system could use automation to ensure that they're placed into the correct department to work in. Let's say; you're going to call the support team if you had a failed hard drive. They'll place it in a token, and people who sponsor hardware equipment will be redirected over here. When you have difficulty accessing another team, and it will work throughout the whole organization, so in this case, the IT service of incident management will be holistic across all employees, and we will use automation to provide support for it.

Keep it simple

Our next guiding principle is keeping it simple and practical. Perhaps you heard this rule many times, i.e. Keep It Simple, Stupid. We are going to discuss it here. I want you to think result in your mind if we talk about this rule. This is what we call the outcome-based approach. If you first start with the outcome, you can go back to all the different phases that you will need to take and to get from the inputs to the results you want to accomplish. We would, therefore, like to use outcome-based approach to generate practical solutions that provide effective end-results with the minimum actions required. But to get there, we must turn back to our fifth guiding rule to look at things from a holistic perspective on the functioning of the organization. I probably won't get a simple and practical method which is going to be effective for our services if I don't know how the organization works. I want to continue with an effortless approach when I first try to build a procedure or a service. We can always add it later, but we have to begin with the smallest number of steps. It means that fewer phases will break down and less progress we have to bring in front of it to see if it truly works for us. I would like you to establish this approach for the most common scenarios as we go through and create it.

For every case, you don't want to seek a solution. Let's say, for example, that you manage the company's service desk. For this business, you run the whole incident management front-end process. When clients call and inform you about their issues, you will check if it best matches just one of three segments. The first segment could be a reset of a password. The second could be that the system won't startup. And the third might be that the network is not accessible to your computer. You may build processes for each of these three most common scenarios. However, not every call will be one of these three situations. Some of you may fall into the fourth category. You wouldn't want to build a solution for every single item. Instead, just build a fourth category that states that if someone calls and asks for one of these items, then the request is managed manually. And then we'll need a person taking charge of it and doing something. While we could finally get something easy for those three scenarios, try to ensure that it is realistic, and automate that approach.

Now we can be conscious, in doing so, of how we will achieve the goals and the results we want. That's the advantage of keeping it simple. You can start quickly by earning fast wins, make sure you have got value, and the simplicity is the supreme sophistication. You really could do things quickly and easily by doing fewer items. This doesn't fall into the three main categories; while using skilled work, you can then focus your team's time on those people. The time for the people involved will be valued. Returning to the resets of passwords, a company with a large service desk of 20, 000 customers, approximately 80 percent of the calls are made due to the reason that people wanted to change and reset their forgotten passwords. So when we developed and streamlined the system, it got automatic and easier for them and gave them greater value, and helped them to work faster.

Moreover, it released most of my work, because they do not attend phone calls anymore from people who try password resets. I can instead take those people and direct them to other things, to the difficult problems that required their attention. It is, therefore, easier to understand and more likely to be noticed, by keeping things simple, and is really the best way to achieve the quick wins and encourages people to adopt what you do.

Service Value Chain

The next important chapter from the exam perspective is the service value chain. We will discuss the fifth major objective in this chapter of the book. It implies that the operations of the value chain and their interconnection need to be understood. There are two sub-goals below this objective. It explains the integrated existence of the service value chain and how it serves the process of value flows and how each value flow operation is meant to be designed. It contains planning, improving, engaging, designing, transitioning, obtaining, constructing and supporting. So we had one internal frame that displayed the value chain to us when we spoke about the service value system. So, we will split that block and look into all its different parts in this lesson. As you will see, we have tasks like participating, planning, enhancing, designing and transformation, gaining, building, providing and supporting goods and services, all of which will work together in the service value chain model.

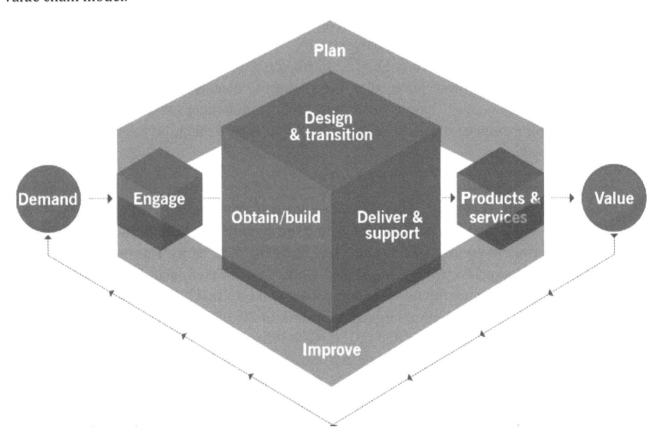

Service Value Chain diagram

Now, when we refer to a model like this, there are a few essential things to know. A sequential chain of events is not shown here. We used to have a Service Development cycle in the ITIL 3 or the older version, which was considered a linear sequence of activities. We used to start with a plan and then move to development, then transformation, and then move to actions. We would then move towards continuous service enhancement and worked through the five development cycles. They no longer exist here in ITIL 4. The series is not sequential. Instead, we usually begin with engagement, but we do not always need to do it, and then depending on it, we will touch other parts of the inner block. And when we explore this main cube, we will see three major groups with the operations in it. We design, change, gain, construct, supply and support. These are the main activities within the value chain of service. And these can coordinate between themselves and other events in every sequence.

This overlap between engaging and the other zones of the service value chain is also another important point to notice. You will see that the section of improve lies in the lower portion of the service value chain. And the overlapping of the purple ribbon extends from improvement to engagement. In this main cube, activities such as delivering and supporting, designing and transformation or obtaining and building are enhanced through this improvement cycle. The improve cycle is linked to our services and products. All are here to demonstrate that the feedback chain lies between each section of the service value chain that goes through the improvement cycle and the continuous improvement of services.

Therefore, the true value of service value chain has to be considered and handled because it will boost the need for the next delivery, the next item, next service or the next upgrade for your products. And, as all these activities are interlinked, it is the reason we called it the service value chain. There are, therefore, many connections between such activities. All of the various steps the company takes to create interest or co-create the service value chain actions will express value. By converting the different inputs into the desired results, all activities are going to contribute to the value chain. And as we use demand and opportunity to do tasks, this crosses the value chain process and gets added value, and then emerges on the other side in the form of the desired result as we want from our services. This is how we look at all this, so to turn these inputs into desired outcomes, these value chain operations will use various combinations of the 34 ITIL procedures that we will discuss in the rest of the book.

Every operation can rely on internal or third party assets; they can examine a variety of procedures, different expertise and capabilities from many of those 34 practices. They don't need to be done separately. They can also be paired. And that is the concept when we get these connections through the operations of the service value chain. The incoming and outgoing communications are all done via the engaging operation of the value chain with all the various entities outside your service provider. This is why it is the first one that usually happens. Whenever you need a new resource, you will get it by obtaining and building activity. Each time you decide to do something, its planning will take place through the planned activity. If you seek to improve things, they are going to pass through the improvement cycle. You got the actual point here. All the various activities we do will be tied into one or more of these multiple containers.

All of this will occur within the main cube for design and transformation, obtaining and building, delivery and support as we produce, change, provide, and maintain and promote a function, service or product. These aren't called as the value chain processes that we recognize as our services and products, our value and our demand. These are linked to our service value system. These are our inputs and end-results. Therefore, the inside of the service chain is what we focus on here. It includes engagement, planning, obtaining and building, delivery and support, as well as design and transformation. Looking at these, we will concentrate on this part of the lesson, and we will move into each section of activities separately as we move forward.

Planning

The first operation in the value chain process we will talk about in this chapter is called planning. It aims to ensure a mutual understanding of the vision, the current situation and the direction of progression across all four aspects of IT service management and all of our organizational products and services. This is your leadership vision; this is where we need to be, and then we have plans to be there. As we consider the input to the planning phase, we must discuss rules, criteria and constraints imposed by the governing structure of the company. We will also aim to integrate all the demands and resources that we obtain from the engagement process in a matter of minutes. We will also focus on all information about the progress of the value chain, improvement programs and strategies given by the cycle of improvement. We will also look at status changes and updates from the improvement phase. We will look at our new and changed services and products from our design and transformation or our processes to acquire and build them.

We will take this information and knowledge from the engagement process on third party service elements. All this will be a part of our planning so we can find out the best way to take our products and services to where we need them to be. It was known once as the strategy if you already know the old ITIL practices. Some of it is also included in this planning program. All these are the inputs to the planning process. What are the outputs of this operation? For that, we will look at three stages of the planning process. First, we have business strategies, the big corporate plans. Then we have tactical planning and operational programs. And that's a sort of big, medium and small as we go deeper. We also have portfolio choices to develop, so we can decide on which services we are going to deliver online to enable us for transformation and design then to develop and build such services and to determine how they can become a reality. When we talk about planning, we focus on the broadway in which we consider how we will get somewhere. We also want to focus on our infrastructures and strategies, and these are the items we can generate and give to design and transformation. So, what do I mean by infrastructures and strategies? So, perhaps part of our plan means that we will use cloud frameworks.

This means that we must not try to build data centres to use design and transformation. We should instead look at the online cloud service providers such as AWS or Microsoft Azure to find things. This would be a choice about architectural design that would go from planning then to design and transformation. Based on our plan, since we want to return things to the improvement process, we can enhance these things as they are possibilities for improvement. Thus, we are going to pass it again from the improvement phase. The service and product selection will also be something we will send to the engagement process. We must create an outline of what we plan to develop and what we want to accomplish in the next three to five years as an organization. When we have the plan of action, we are passing it down to the engagement process. We will then engage with clients, buyers and service suppliers to see how we can get the desired output from this plan. And this engagement can occur through contracting or connecting to get what we need, which takes us to the last thing.

Engagement will be a result of our plans and the contracts, and the agreements will be enforced to bring this into the design and transformation phase, then it passes to the building team so that they can develop what we are thinking. That is the idea here. When you learn about planning within the service value chain, I need you to consider the fact that we are talking about big plans. We think of road maps. For example, I have a road map in my organization which states that we will support you in various training lessons and produce videos and tests for the next few years. We will not make any effort to do it if it is not on the road map, because this is our strategy, and this is what we are about to do. It is our huge, overall strategic plan. We now have a tactical approach out of this strategic plan which says we might be doing these three training courses in the next year. After that, we will do operational planning to design one of these training courses. And it passes from the big plan to a medium plan, and then to the very comprehensive operating strategy. This is the premise when we are discussing plans within the value chain of services.

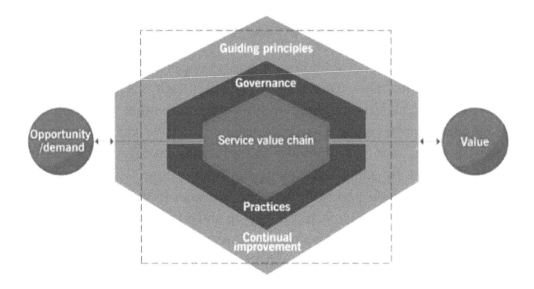

Improve

The next thing I want to concentrate on is the improvement activity of the value chain. The objective of improving the value chain operation is to continuously improve our goods, services and procedures for all our value chain activities and the four IT services management aspects. In order to improve operation, we need many different inputs. We will look at things such as information on products and services enhancement that will obtain from our delivery and support process. The delivery and support refer to your operational staff when we talk about it. It is they who manage the help desk and operate all the databases and utilities. They receive continuous feedback from your end-users, clients and buyers. We also need to receive feedback from shareholders from the engagement process. If we look at it, it could be between our distributors and us or our investors and us or between our clients and us. All the information gets back through the engagement phase and passes on to improvement activity which you will use to enhance your services so that you can improve on that feedback.

We also want to examine the facts on the efficiency of all different value chain operations and the possibilities for improvement. We want to ensure things are transferred directly to the improvement phase as we measure things across the production cycle and all our activities. So we can find out how we can do things better easier, quicker, and more effective regardless of the case. We still strive to improve in order to achieve higher value at lower costs. We would also like to analyze all the information on our current and improved goods and services from design and transformation to obtain / construction. As we are building a new database or a service, we want the data to be collected and transferred back to improvement phase, because we can then improve and make suggestions on how to do this more accessible, quicker, faster, etc. We will also analyze all the information about our company's third-party resources from the engagement view. The improvement also gathers information from the engagement process, from our stakeholders and vendors, as our supplier could switch from self-hosting architecture to a cloud-based infrastructure.

And this new information will lead to our future development planning. If we discuss the results from the improve phase, they would be improvement programs and strategies for all other aspects of the value chain. The improvement comes into play across the whole service value chain and value system. By looking at that, the improvement team will find out and instruct the building and obtaining team that if you did x things, you guys might have achieved it for half that price. And they will give them some suggestions or strategy to improve it next time. We will also have details from the plan and the governing body about the value chain performance. When we collect the information, we will pass it on to those people and ensure that we can use it to enhance data in the field. We will also look at our improve progress reports for all operations of the value chain. Since we have gathered all the information from everyone and find a way to improve it, we will reschedule these progress reports and say, these are the suggestions, and how you can improve things.

 It's the whole concept of continuous improvement repeatedly. We will not give it directly to consumers, service providers or any of our suppliers when it comes to our suggestions for agreements and contracts. Instead, we will pass it back to engage, as it will lead us to all those external agencies. This is how we will do it with any service agreement and contract advancements. And finally, for design and transformation, we have our performance data of service. We will also move all information back into design and transition, to help design and transform better services next time as we get all this information and look at how we can enhance it. All of this goes back to the end of the continuous improvement. When we think about the improvement phase in the value chain process, we need to know how to make things better, fast, affordable, simpler, and better functionality. Regardless of any case, still, we can improve and achieve better results, which is the central concept of this phase.

Engage

The objective of engaging in the value chain is to provide with a good knowledge of the investor requirements, to guarantee sustained interaction with the shareholders. Also, to foster good visibility and better relations with them. If we talk about engagement, it is both internal and external in our company. So when I think about the various inputs for the engagement here, I take the portfolio of products and services that I will obtain from the plans. When I obtain the services and products portfolio, then I can think of who to engage with? Who wants the new roadmap to know? Who should know that a new brand is hitting the market? Who should know what they can offer in this service or a portion of it? This is the whole concept there, which communicates to your partners inside and outside the organization. We will also search for inputs for a high demand rate of products and services. We generally see these things from our clients, and we listen to them and what they want to engage in them.

Let's say if I have 50 students who are contacting me and asking me that they want me to offer the service of cloud certification. I will start listening to develop this certificate, and bring it in our schedule and move it through the whole lifecycle. All rely on the need for our products and services, and that's what we listen to our clients. One reason for offering other certifications could be that many of my ITIL students have asked me that they want a certificate for project management, will I be offering it. So we can go for it due to the sufficient demand. Let's consider we did it. The other input is your clients ' requests and suggestions. We ask you for comments and suggestions after you complete this book. If the client tells us that the author speaks about his examples too much, we will use fewer cases next time we build a new lesson.

Over the years, we have received a lot of this sort of reviews, and we can adjust and improve things according to these feedbacks, and we always do it. With your IT infrastructure, you want to do the same thing. You always want your customers to give reviews and then you can produce and deliver a better item with this feedback. Next, we would also like to address your end-users ' incidents, service demands and suggestions. That could be different from your buyers. In my case, my buyers are my users, but if we consider this form a wide-ranging IT sense, I could have a client buying service for hundreds of users. In this situation, I have to think differently from the client level and consumer-level about the reviews. It allows you to find out what you are doing right if you get all this feedback, and then you can pass this information on to the improvement phase so that it can be used in enhancement plans. We also have information about completing help desk support tasks from delivery and support. That will be out next input. Delivery and support are one of the main factors for which your engage will work closely.

At this level, your service desk plays a role in delivery and support. This is where your activities take place. That is where you will reach out, touch and get the feedback and reviews directly from your end-users. So it is very important to be able to look at this and bring this information back into the engagement cycle through delivery and support, and then accessing the other areas of the service value chain. Furthermore, we want to reflect the input of our investment opportunities. Looking at the market, and looking at the requirements, we will find out what our present situation looks like. It's a coordinated and interconnected effort. Then we have our information from vendors and partners about our third-party service elements. We have this again in the engagement activity, just like we did previously. We will also make sure that the entire lifecycle and the delivery and support staff provides information about services and products. As we receive that, we can arrange it and then drive it over all the different parts and activities in the service value chain. We also have our programs and strategies for improvement.

We're supposed to get them from improvement activity. And what are we supposed to do with them as engagement staff? Well, we'll tell people about it. Hey, students, on Z day, we will improve the lessons and publish a new book. We get this out of our plans, and we advertise it to our clients, our users and our investors. Finally, we would also like to get progress reports from improving activity. Again, as part of our engagement, we will share this information. I want to talk about saying something to others when I am speaking about engagement. I interact and communicate with someone. So what are some of the results when we're talking about engagement? Okay, our demands and resources are integrated. When we gather all of this information from the industry and our clients, we will now reverse, integrate it and bring it into planning cycle so that they can include that in our overall strategies. We will also look at our services and products needs and give them to design and transformation in order to provide clients with better services.

To provide end-users everything they need, we also take in customer feedback and demands and supply them to support and delivery phase. Therefore, if you come to engage in our business as a student and you tell us that you require more lecture notes, then we can give it into the design and transform cycle that can create them. Then you can pass it to obtain and build process where it gets buildup then you can send it to delivery and support which is sent to you as a client. And it works as they interrelate these processes. We will also have an output of possibilities for improvement as well as feedback from shareholders, as we gather everything because we interact with all of these external groups, we will take this and pass it on to improvement cycle or activity so that they can work on it. We also receive things like change or requests for product initiatives, all of which we shall receive, centralize hem and forward to obtain / building process. Once again, contracts, law and partnerships are being done.

To obtain, build and design and transform, the agreements and contracts from the direct and indirect suppliers must turn over to get the services and goods on which these contracts depend. We will also analyze the performance of our third-party service elements because we have collected all of these data, but we will not do much with them as the engagement team. We need to pass it to people who plan, the design and transformation team, the people who get and build, as well as the people in delivery and support. They all need this data, and we are the people who collect it, so it's our responsibility to pass it on.

And finally, the services efficiency reports were one thing we collected. We have this data from all parts of the service, and we wish to inform our customers of it now. The availability of our product as measured by A, B and C is 99 per cent. Let me tell the clients about this report so that they know what they get. It's the idea in engagement. Engage is the glue that operates the whole system. All communication happens through it. Things are brought in, they are processed and brought out, to and from various activities, procedures, clients, shareholders, end-users and service providers and partners. All this happens because it's focused on engagement. All the people are responsible for the communication.

Design and Transition

Design and transition/transformation is the next operation of the value chain we will be discussing. The aim of the design and transformation value chain process is to ensure that the services and products continuously satisfy the shareholder's quality, cost and time expectations on the market. Here we will ensure that we find out how this item will be constructed. Here we get all the layouts for it, and then determine how we transfer it from a concept to being developed and placed into the market. The design and transformation process has many different inputs. We have to take portfolio choices from the field of planning when we begin to talk about design and transformation. We would also like to ensure that we understand the framework and strategies established by the planning phase. We will also take things from the phase of engagement, such as service and product demands from clients and users as well as from other sectors. We also want to ensure that we consider the enhancement programs and plans resulting from the improvement phase.

We will also look at all the progress reports from the improvement phase so that we can find out how we can build it better the next time around? We will also discuss all of our knowledge about service efficiency that comes from our service delivery and support and improve procedures. Are we achieving the defined service targets? Have we efficiently transitioned anything? All this is something that we have to take into account as we develop and transition our services from the ideas and planning into a usable product that can be provided to a customer for usage. All this takes place within this area of design and transformation. If we look at this, then we will also focus on certain items, such as which service elements are usable, that come from the process of obtaining and building. Obtaining and building process has already many things built in. Perhaps we can recycle some of the stuff we already have and use when we design a new product or service. Perhaps we can reuse some of the already existing items when we design a new product and utilize them in our new program. Finally, information and knowledge must be considered. Now, information and knowledge will come from two separate areas.

Next, we have information and knowledge about third-party service elements from the engagement process. This is where we'll decide what material is appropriate for usage as we did in obtain and build phase, but now we approach it from a third-party or vendor's point of view. We will be able to help design and transform something better to operate around the capability by actually knowing that our vendor has this sort of potential. Information and knowledge of new and improved goods and services is the other part of this process. We will get this from our obtaining and building process. As we build and get things, we will be able to obtain product details, known failures and other related data, all of which can be used as an input to this design and transformation activity. So, as far as its outputs are concerned, we will look at things such as the specifications and the needs, and we will pass them on to obtain and build. Therefore, I have to find out what the demands and specifications are, as I created this brand new product to satisfy my students.

Then pass it to those who buy servers, purchase integrations and buy technology for automation which will allow this to happen inside the process of obtaining and build. We will also go and pass that on to engagement if we have to contract anything. We have to provide them with the terms of the contract and the agreement that we require to enter into service level contracts, managed services pacts and other procurement and supplier agreements, and deliver them by engaging with these external parties. Another output is any new and improved services and products which we will be able to obtain from the design and transformation process, and we will pass these on to delivery and support. When we start discussing knowledge and information, as we get it and other improved services or new products, it will be transferred to obtain and build process. Not only to this process but all various parts of the value chain operations, because it's necessary to know what iterations two or three will look like. When planning the next edition, we will pass it over to design and transformation.

We have to pass on the things to obtain and build process so that they can build them according to your design. You have to move it on to delivery and support phase so that when it fails, they can sustain it. The information and knowledge about new or improved items are needed in all value chain operations. And ultimately, we want to ensure that we obtain knowledge about performance and possibilities for enhancement through design and transformation phase, and then back to the improvement phase. When we move through and design/build service, we will find that we have got three issues as we attempt to develop any system. We must pass it to improvement phase so that they can discover ways of improving and making our systems more effective. So, when we begin to learn about the design and transformation as an operation, consider taking an idea from the plans and what will be developed in the obtain/built process. This is the primary focus here. Still, for this operation, there are all these other inputs and outputs, because these are non-sequentially occurring and things always happen in fast development as we deal with IT infrastructure.

Build

Obtain/build is our next activity in the value chain process. The aim of this value chain operation is now to ensure that service elements are accessible whenever they are needed and that the negotiated demands are met. If I m building service, I have to build it according to the design specifications given to me by the design and transformation activities. Now, when it gets down to obtain/build, there are many different inputs and outputs. As we speak about inputs, we will get them from various sources.

Let's first talk about the policies and architectures. They come out of the plans as we have already discussed them many times. Plans generate architectures and policies, and many of these chains of value use them. If we understand the concept of governance, our organization's architecture and policies, they surely help us to design and transition a better customer service. And, we know what it means to obtain/build it under those specifications. We'll look next at agreements and contracts. When we have contracts and agreements with direct and indirect vendors and stakeholders, they will all be used as an input from engagement to obtain and build phase. We will also analyze products and services and the direct and indirect vendors, and stakeholders are going to provide them. Again, we will have some good product or service once we have subscribed for it. The data, communication and the engagement are all obtained from the contract's engage part, but the physical provision and receipt of the service elements, products and services lie within the obtain/build part of this operation. And that will lead us to what we want to create or develop, which will get the needs and specifications for it.

From where can we get the specifications and demands? Well, design and transformation phase will provide it. Someone built this service, and they gave us these models here in the obtain and build process, where we will download the program, buy our servers, get everything connected and integrated, and then convert it into a real living world when it comes back to design and transform. Another input to this value chain activity in enhancement programs and strategies that will come from improving operation as the enhanced behaviour has looked at how to make them better? When they find out the procedures and systems by which we can improve things, they will get that back to build them from build/obtain process. Our progress reports on improvement are yet another thing that we get from improvement activity. Again, they will examine our procedures, our practices, the lessons they have studied before and will help us improve our way of doing business. Now we'll get something out of it again by returning to our engagement activity. We will make changes and start project requests, as if you have any issues with a service, you could add it in a change request as a client or a buyer or an end-user. And if you ask for a change request, it comes in from engagement activity because it is an external interaction.

Once that request is received in engagement activity, it will be processed and then passed on to us in obtain/build activity so that we can acquire or create the new service to meet that consumer's requirement. Certain requests for improvements from delivery and support may also be received. The people who supply and support things, let's say, there has been a switch malfunction, so, the delivery and support would make a change request that says that switch number two must be changed. Thus, we'd get a new switch in the obtain/build phase by replacing the old switch with a new one. Again, all these procedures are interconnected. Then we get to our information and knowledge process. We have already discussed much of these two terms. Design and transformation activity provides information and knowledge on new products and improved services. We have to know what we're going to design and transformation to a new service so we can build on it.

And another thing that comes from a third-party service element is information and knowledge. This information will also come from engagement, as engagement will push this out and obtain it from third-party vendors. Let's focus on the outputs now, as we learned about all the inputs. Service elements are one of the outputs for our delivery and support. I will create various components when I decide to build a service. I might create a specific server or program or computer software. It's not my concern as obtaining/building once I develop it and it goes into live-action. It is now transferred to delivery and support activity where they will run it regularly to provide the end-users with everything they require. This will contain spare pieces, reusable items, new features, devices and software. All this content can be given to delivery and support. Normally, if it is something huge like a new system or a new application, it goes from obtaining/building up to transform phase, then from here, it passes to delivery and support. However, when it is small such as a spare piece or a reusable item, then it doesn't have to be designed and transformed again.

Instead, it will go into delivery and support straight away. For example, let's assume I've created a new cloud service, and we need to get it out in the live environment. We got the models from design and transformation phase, and then we developed it here in obtain/build. Once we've designed it, we'll send it back to design and transformation. So that it can be shifted into the live environment, and from there it will return to delivery and support. You could see the connections between all these procedures and activities. Information and knowledge of our new and improved service elements is another output from this operation, and this is an output for all other value chain operations. Whenever I'm building something new, I have to tell everybody so that they've got the features, the capability, how long it lasts, when it has to be updated or fixed, as well as we can plan it, model, it, and fund it. All other operations will use this information and knowledge, and that is why it is essential to have a good knowledge management system.

When we come back to agreements and contracts, we will send all the details and demands we have to the engagement phase, where they will communicate with the external shareholders, partners, and vendors. And eventually, in the obtain/build phase, we will receive all the information about our activities. And we will collect the service performance reports and enhancement possibilities, and transfer them to the improvement activity. In this way, they can organize everything and look at all actions holistically and see how they can improve themselves further. So I want you to think about it very clearly when we're talking about the value chain operations of obtaining and building. If we buy and install something, that's part of this obtain and building. If we program something and create a new product, it will come inside obtain/build. It is when the service or product is built, developed and coded depending on the design and transformation requirements. You will pass it on to design and transformation once it's ready, so to officially transfer it to delivery and support phase. And in the case of something minor like repairing switches or hardware, that will go to delivery and support, which we'll be learning in the next section.

Delivery and support

Delivery and support is our third operation in the middle of the value chain process. That's where many of us work in the IT industry. If you work in IT support, you may be working within the delivery and support department. Its objective is to ensure that the products are supplied and supported according to negotiated criteria and shareholder preferences in the value chain process. It's like a service process that I'll talk about. We want to ensure that the end-user receives the quality service and support he/she requires, so we call it delivery and support. I will provide some capability and end-user support. In the case of this book, you are using the delivery and support procedure while you read one of its chapters. We offer you this content, and we also support you if you have got any problem. It is part of the service. Now, when we are creating our next manuscript, we would return to design and transformation. When we create and edit that next manuscript, it is obtained and build, but once we've it done and you're able to read it, it got delivered and supported, and the same thing works for our information technology services.

When I build a new server for the emails, it is obtained/build. When it's out, and you use this e-mail server, we get into delivery and support phase. So what about the delivery and support inputs? All the new and improved services and products which are delivered by design and transformation are its first inputs. Note that the process of obtaining and the building will develop it, move it back into transformation so that it can be positioned on the market efficiently. Then delivery/support will operate it from there. We will also have agreements and contracts with direct and indirect vendors and shareholders made available to us from engagement. Because engage involves all the external commitments, we will use those agreements to get what we need in delivery and support. We will also get service elements through obtaining and build. As the new email server is created, it will be transferred, and we will finally get it in delivery and support. Then, we will achieve things such as enhancements programs and strategies that come out of the process of improvement, or our activities in the value chain. The status updates from increased value chain operation will also be provided to us. We'll get help desk support tasks from it as well because it is an engagement function whenever we talk to a client. And we will also take the information and knowledge. We get all the details and information on our latest and improved system elements and services from the design and transformation phase, or from obtain/build. On the other hand, the information on the service elements from third parties is taken from our engaged partners. This is the way that we get things into this operation of the value chain process.

On the other hand, we will now output other things such as the support we provide to our clients and consumers. That's what you're using. If you visit the website, then you are in the delivery/support cycle as you profit from the distribution. You will also get knowledge outputs on the execution of help desk support tasks. Therefore, if you have a question and have a service ticket, you will get a report to you at some stage through the phase of engagement that means the complaint has been solved and the answer has been identified here. One thing you will get is service and product quality data that comes from the engage and improvement operations, just like the other value chain activities. All this must be returned to the end-user. We will also output items such as enhancement possibilities. And when we find out that the way we produce our book content is not the best, perhaps we should try another one. We will send the enhancement suggestion and opportunity over to improve, and then it can integrate that, focus on that and see how we can change ourselves in the long run.

The engage value chain operation also involves the enhancement of the agreements and partnership specifications. And if we look at the various demands for changes, all of those that come in to produce, we can export them to obtain/build, so that they can get and create the item and modify it in the manner we need it. All of the above processes are interlinked. All of them go in and out pretty much all the time. The service quality data is the last output we have for the delivery and related operations. We must collect a great deal of information about our services. For example, we may want to find out how much space we spent on a shared drive or the throughput, availability, or the power or the quality of servers. This is all about service quality data, and as we gather all this information, we will analyze it and move it on to the design and transformation level.

Why would it be designed and altered? They always look at what capability you have, and do you require more? For example, if we have a single database server and we began to see that the trend was 80-90%, we would like to ensure that we build the upgraded version of that database server with extra capacity. Perhaps it switches to a cloud infrastructure, or it may move to an environment that has several sites, or it uses a network for content delivery. Whatever that is, it needs to be created, and thus by refilling the service quality data back to design and transformation, it can allow us to build the next iteration of our service.

Continual improvement

We spent a great deal of time in each layer of the service value system. As we know the middle layer of SVS is known as the value chain process, which is discussed in the previous segment. Now we will discuss its lower portion, which is the continuous improvement or continual enhancement. In the SVS diagram, you can see that the outermost, purple layer is labelled as continual improvement. So, there is a block of procedures called practices, just above the continuous improvement layer, and these activities will be the 34 different ITIL practices that we will address in the rest of the book.

Interestingly, continuous improvement is one of these 34 practices. Why does the diagram display continuous improvement as its activity, apart from the fact that it is practice? Well, because it is so necessary to constantly improve in every aspect of the IT service management process. We must always try to improve everything we do. And if we analyze this from the perspective of the test, there are two occurrences of continuous improvements. First, the objective of the continuous improvement process needs to be recalled. Note the recall keyword here. This means that you must be able to learn that, word by word, and define its meaning during the test.

Second, it is also necessary to discuss how the continuous improvement and enhancement model works into the value chain and value system. We will be talking specifically about the continuous improvement process in this section of the book. I asked you to recall its meaning now, so what is the definition? So, the objective of this activity is to get the company's processes and products into line with increasing business requirements through ongoing procedures. Such procedures include defining and improving services, service elements, activities or features of effective and productive service administration. This is a very long description, but you have to learn it because you have to use the right words if they ask you something in fill-in-the-blanks. You should be able to identify it as a continuous process of improvement when they give you this description. This is the amount of information you require for the recall portion of the test. Now, as we go over this section, I can show you how the continuous improvement template fits into the value chain activity so that you can understand it and illustrate it during the test, and follow each step of that model.

What is the vision?

Every improvement program should hold up the objectives and aims of the organization. The first step of a model of continuous improvement is to describe the program's vision. What are we trying to achieve precisely? This will provide the framework for all our future choices and tie our decisions to the future vision of the company. The vision must emerge from your top management. It should come from the C-suite, the President, the CFO, the CIO, or somebody else who has this executive viewpoint of where we are going with the company. Two key areas are focused on this phase of the continuous improvement model. First, the vision and the goals of an organization need to be transferred to specific business divisions, agencies, groups and people. We then take this framework and extract it from the larger organization to put our improvement programs into particular cases. If we do not, it will be hard for us to know that we are going in the right direction. Secondly, you need a high-level vision for the expected improvement, and this must be developed. Someone must write it, and it must be approved.

Usually, if it's an organizational large improvement project, it will be your head of department or upper management. Now you may think why this step is so important to determine your vision? So, if we fail to do this, in some places or groups, we might see some incremental changes, but we won't see any entire company's holistic improvements. You must have a great vision if you want huge changes. Now the other thing is that sometimes these changes we are focusing on do not always lead to advancing the overall organization vision. Instead, we could spend more time and money, resources and energy on applying non-value operations to projects because we had no idea about real vision. And if we only realized what the vision was, we could have spent all those assets much better in other improvements. Therefore, when you finish the vision stage of the model, you can make sure you know what the high-level path is and understand it entirely. You will ensure that you also identify and understand the context of the proposed improvement programs within the company.

Furthermore, you need to define all your shareholders and understand their positions well. You must also be aware of the position of the person or group responsible for this change now. And you will understand their role in realizing the overall company's vision and also agree on the planned value from this vision. We all could know how we get into that. Ultimately, when we realize our true vision, we will know which path to take for all our improvements. So, who we will support with this, and who will help us and how it will affect the entire organization?

Where are we now?

A clear and precise understanding of the base point and the effect of your program can decide how successful an improvement plan is. Now, if you consider an improvement as a path from point x to y, the step indicates how x point looks like. Think about this in a way, when I told you to come to my office today, you would first have to learn two things. You must know first where my workplace is, and I am in the New York zone. Secondly, you have to know where you are right now. You will need to get into your car and drive to my office in case you are in Los Angeles. But you'll have to hire a ship or catch a plane and then go west if you are in London, England. Based on where you come from, will decide where you will go and how you will get there. If you don't know what your base point is, your path actually cannot be figured out. For our IT services, we must know the existing condition of our products and services. So, we will perform a current evaluation of the operating services to determine the client's view of value for our services.

So, what are our staff's current skills and what methods and practices are needed in providing these services? We could even look at our current databases, our networks and other tools for their functional capabilities. When you look at the capacity of your company to provide products, you will also analyze the environment and behaviour of your company's employees. So, with all this, we will carry out this evaluation to assess the current status with the help of objective analysis whenever possible. Now, an objective analysis is anything we can calculate. It's not like this; do I have a good feeling or a bad feeling about it? We will try to give the numbers there. Such measurements are used for establishing a benchmark. In later stages of the process, this baseline can be used to evaluate our success against our actual baseline or current condition. Please note, if you never find out where you began from, it is hard to track and calculate the success of your enhancement programs. Until going to the next level of the continuous improvement model, make sure that you take the time to establish a good target baseline.

Where do we want to be?

As we step out of stage two, we know where we are in our baseline. Now the question arises, where are we going to be? Let's say you have returned to your university. You had a dream when you started the first year. This is stage one. So you dreamed that you would score a 3.5 GPA. Your first semester has just ended, and your scores are here. You did not do as you thought, sadly, and you got some B and C grades. You are now staring at your GPA, and you see that you have gained 2.8. Where we are now, as this is the second stage? We are at a 2.8 GPA. Now, you have to decide if next semester will be better then we will go and try to improve things if you have taken this decision. You may study deeper or longer. So you agreed that you want to have a 3.5 GPA by the end of this academic year. And you plan to have an overall 3.5 GPA vision by the end of the next academic year. In step three, this is what we will do. We must decide, both in the near as well as the future, where we want to be. We will conduct a gap evaluation during this phase. This will look at our overall picture, where we are at the moment and where we want to go.

Based on this evaluation, we will be able to identify this delta and that gap. Let's say, I wanted to see a thousand bucks in my bank account, but today I have only a hundred dollars, so the difference is 900 dollars. One thousand bucks, where I want to go, compared to the $100 I have right now. So, we will find a way to get 900 dollars more. Now, it is typically not financial in the case of our IT services. However, it is based on some important factors. This will be based on CSFs or KPIs. The CSF stands for critical success factor, and KPI means key performance indicator. In any case, we usually refer to these as metrics in the world of business. These are the measures we will use to measure things and to find out what the gap is. Now, it must be remembered that our vision from stage one may be aspiring and won't be accomplished.

The reason is that our vision sometimes goes beyond what we can do. Let's take another example of our university GPA. Let us assume that your dream had a university degree with a score of 4.0 GPA. Based on our current status that we have noticed in phase 2, we will never be able to achieve this 4.0 because our overall GPA is already falling due to some B's and some C's in the transcript. We can now hold our dream of 4.0 CGPA, but we know that we will never achieve it. Perhaps we can hit 3.7, but never 4.0. That's how logic works. So now, in phase 3, we will create some other targets that we can accomplish by trying to come closer to the actual goal whether or not we get that goal in the end. Now in phase 3, we will find out where we want to go and set our targets. We must comply with the main performance metrics, such as KPIs and CSFs. But we haven't done anything yet to improve at this stage significantly. Our goals have just been set. But, that's all right as in next step, phase four; we will start formulating our strategy in order to take actions.

Take action

Now, it's time for some actions. We've got our vision, our starting point, our objectives, and our strategy. We will now take action in step five and implement those strategies. If you want to take action, you can do so under the typical waterfall method, in which a huge improvement program is split into stages, it got arranged and organized, and a drastic change takes place over a short period, and you move to a new process. This may help if you need to remove and upgrade an old system. However, most of the time, you would certainly take steps using an agile approach with less iteration. In this situation, you can improve your services and products less often, but you will gain steady but larger benefits and profits. Both strategies can work, and it quite depends on the scenario you use. During this project, your goal progress must be constantly measured; the risk during these changes controlled and the transparency and knowledge of the program must be constantly sprayed across the organization, so everyone knows what is taking place. When the enhancement program is done, we will continue to phase six and see whether or not we have progressed.

How to keep the momentum?

Our 7th and last step are to decide how we sustain our momentum. We have undoubtedly been spending a great deal of time, a lot of money and a lot of work hours to enhance everything in the company. When we achieve our goal, we don't want to rest, but we want to progress more, yes, because we always want to improve ourselves. And if we haven't achieved our goal, we need to re-adjust and find out how to grow in order to achieve our targets. If we did it, we could go back to a previous phase, create a new target, develop a new strategy and then start again. But for a couple of minutes, let's think positive. Let us consider that we have accomplished our targets in phase three with our key performance metrics and key success factors. Everything is going good. We've evolved, and we're all grateful. Even when we don't do anything, people will return to their old business methods and techniques. For instance, perhaps the satisfaction rate of our customer support was not very high, so we have launched an enhancement program, which lifted our ratings by 50%. We then chose to focus on a new program, and guess now what?

Since the customer care programs are no longer closely monitored, the call centre operators stop trying hard, and the satisfaction ratings begin to drop again. Now that's the reverse of what we want. When we performed the program so well in one department, we chose to keep the momentum going by pushing the transition through several divisions and issuing a new corporate policy. In any case, we want to ensure that the progress continues and that we keep up to the change we are making. It's all included in stage seven. It's about developing and executing a plan to maintain the positive momentum and to hold us on the track to further progress. And then you will see that we are back to the top of the model once again in the diagram. Why is that? Well, because we would always like to change. This is our objective, constantly improving. This is a cyclical model. We keep going all around, again and again, increasing efficiency, productivity and quality as we go forward. Here in the continuous model of improvement, this is the whole purpose. We want to continue to improve.

General Management Practices

Categories of practices:

We will discuss all 34 of the ITIL 4 practices in the next three segments of the book. The three categories of these 34 different practices are general management practices, the practice of managing services and the practice of technical management. But what exactly is a practice? That raises the question. You may recall that there was a section of the diagram that mentioned these practices from our service value system lecture. A practice is a collection of coordinated tools designed to accomplish or attain a goal. Each practice supports several service value chain operations and contains tools based on the four IT service management aspects. We will concentrate on the first 14 ITIL 4 practices in this portion of the book. Such practices are known as general management. However, let me tell you what you should know for the certification test before diving into these general management techniques because, in the next three segments, we will cover a great deal of information. First, the objectives of these ITIL practices must be known.

I won't list all of these practices right now, but I will tell you whether you should remember them for the examination or not because we cover each practice in their sections. However, you must remember the definitions of these 15 practices, as these are at the reminder level of knowledge for the examination. As a recall, ITIL 4 contains 34 practices. As I cover each of these practices briefly, this will at least help you to get an outline of each of these 34; you need only to learn fifteen of them for the basic exam level. Six of these 15, needs to be more deeply learned. Again I must inform you that these things are very critical when I discuss them and what you need to give more emphasis than just understanding the term. We will first discuss all the methods that you must learn in detail as we start with each of the areas covering various types of practices. Then we will learn those practices for which the definition will be remembered. Then we will finish each portion with practices, which are not part of the fundamental exam and are covered purely for your general knowledge. As we go over these three portions of the book, we will also discuss the seven terms which are in the reminder stage of the exam and which we will address during our discussion of those practices. It includes the IT resource, event, setup item, change, incident, issue and known mistake. I must inform you once more when we learn them in the lectures; these are the terminologies of which you must remember the meanings. Let's get into the practices of general management.

Management practices

We will discuss the general management Techniques in this portion of the book, as it is the first of three types of idle practices. We will discuss 14 of the 34 practices in this section. First, we'll learn about continuous improvement, and you've got to understand that deeply. Then we will discuss management of information security, relation and supply management. These three are the reminder level of knowledge, so you must memorize their meaning. And the other ten practices will also be covered in this category, and they will be for your general knowledge only.

For the test, you don't have to learn them, which included architecture management, information management, measurement and reporting management of organizational transformation, portfolio management, project management, risk management, financial services management, policy and management of staff and talent. Such general principles for management services for more general business areas have now been accepted and modified. We use portfolio management and project management in every IT business organization. We use them in all professional associations, and this is why they are called general fields of management in companies, and that's why we include them here in this section.

Continuous Improvement

The first approach in general management is continuous improvement and this one you should know in detail in this chapter for the test. For this, you must be able to describe continuous improvement, its objective, and how it fits in the value chain process. Therefore, we address continuous improvement by constantly identifying and enhancing the service, service elements, processes or any other factor of effective and secure services and products management. So, how can we improve things? It's all about continuous improvement. Now, there are a couple of key aspects that we should know about continuous improvement. First, we need to promote the company's continued enhancement. We always want to be larger, stronger, faster, affordable or more productive. The second important role of continuous improvement is to ensure its time and budgets. In an organization, it's really easy to continue to focus on the same issues every day and not care about changing them. We want to ensure that our time and resources are secured so that we can continue to improve our processes.

Then we need to focus on the improved possibilities for identification and logging. Whenever you work on a service, you may have a thought and say, if we were doing the Z way, it would be easier. We want to log it down at this point, define it, and we could eventually get back to it so it can progress further. Another thing we want to remember is the way we evaluate and give priority to possibilities for change. You might have many wonderful ideas, but what should we focus on first? This is part of ongoing progress. We want to learn about how we can explain such enhancement steps in a business case. You have to get a budget to improve yourself at a certain point. Therefore, you will need to think about how we can do that and make the case of it for the upper management or executives. Perhaps you'll suggest something like this to your boss that we should apply this improvement activity. It will take us 28 hours to make it straight away, but it could save us 12 hours per week.

So we'll cover up the time in just two weeks. This is a good idea. This is an example of how to do a business case. Next, we want to discuss how these enhancements should be designed and implemented and how we will assess and analyze these improvements and their outcomes. Also, we addressed this lot in the last part of the chapter as we learned about the model of continuous improvement. This is only the standard practice that this model can work. We also want to ensure that our enhancement actions are organized throughout the organization. Note that we want to think and work holistically for the maximum improvement throughout the enterprise. There is a range of various tools that can now be applied to our toolbox as we deal with continuous changes. These tools are processes, frameworks and tactics. These are things like sleek approaches in which we try to minimize waste and dual-phase programs that we attempt to organize and gradually improve the way we do things. We could do maturity tests to see how experienced our company is and how successful we are?

We could use dev operations in such a way that we can produce and commercialize things earlier and better. We may use a balanced scoreboard, look at the progress, look at the lens of all four different aspects of service management, and how do we plan it? This is our idea, indeed. Let's consider an example of a CIR here. Here, you see that three different things are identified, with a medium and high effect for each of them. And then there's the last section where we're going to say how we use it. So, we will build this program, and in the first quarter of next year, we will launch it. And we want to ensure we capture it whatever the strategy is. The last thing I want to talk about in continuous improvement is how this works when you consider improving partnerships continuously. We want to bring this in like a pyramid. So we start from below and begin to think of our stakeholders and vendors. How can we strengthen relationships with our vendors and stakeholders? So, we can do that by evaluating our contracts and calculating, reporting and enhancing these procedures.

Then the next primary target we have is the interior of our company. From there, we want to try to participate actively as a central part of everybody's task in continuous enhancement programs. When it comes to this, continuous improvement is not the task of the constant improvement supervisor. It's the responsibility of every member of the company. And so we have a special team for continuous improvement tasks in the company which is led by its manager. Their job is to lead the activities throughout the company and advocate for the practice. They are the ones who get other people to participate in the fight and to contribute to our progress. And then we have those few senior members at the top of the pyramid, who will try to steadily improve people's way of thinking and working of continuous advancement by giving the right direction. And so this reminds us of the continual model of improvement we've heard about. When we look at this hierarchy, and instead, we do it from top to bottom; we start to see the founders coming up with the dream, which is the origin of our continuous improvement framework.

Then we have our unit of continuous improvement the team that will evaluate where we are and decide where we want to be. They will also help to formulate the plans. But then, if we're going to act, we need to do this with everyone in the company, even stakeholders and vendors outside the company. Then we'll reevaluate where we all are, and then find out how we keep going and how we do it all. You can see how everything links together again and again. Now the last thing I want to think about is how it interacts with the various activities of the value chain. So if we analyze how continuous improvements are going to work within our plans, all planning processes will be continuously enhanced. We must look at the tools and techniques and ensure they are all related to the current goal of the company and the framework in which we work. Once we begin to look from the viewpoint of improvement, this value chain process depends on the continuous improvement method.

It's all about getting better. It integrates our services and activities to enhance them at every level of the organization and throughout the service value system. Now that we focus on the rest of the value chain and its operations of engagement, design and transformation, obtain/build, and delivery and support, we are continually improving each one, as our policies, procedures and processes are continuously enhanced. And all of these are related to the continuous improvement process itself. As you can see, for all we do in ITIL 4, the continuous improvement approach is there. We always try to improve. We always do. If we go back to the value chain, you can see that all those inner cubes and the engagement with this purple line are touched by improvement. This is because each of them has its influence. Here the aim is to continually improve, as we never want to stop changing, which is a key to the success of ITIL 4.

Information Security Management

The management of information security is our next general practice. You just have to remember the concept of the information security management practice for the test. And this definition means that the administration of information security is there to secure the information the company needs to manage its operations. But what is the management of information security? Okay, it's all about knowledge and management of the privacy, integrity, accessibility, verification and non-repudiation risks. When you think this way, information security is all about data protection. We want to avoid spammers' attacks and breaches of data. We want to ensure that our data is kept secure and that it is safe from potential threats if we talk about privacy. We normally do this by encoding the data so that someone can't go into it, hack it and view it. As we speak of our data integrity, we want to ensure our information does not alter in the transition process, or use, or storage.

To do this, we typically perform a hashing function against the information, which gives us a digital fingerprint so we can see if a malicious attacker has changed a file or not. As we talk about accessibility or availability, we are considering things such as ensuring that the user can get access to their data whenever it is needed So, if I have a website that is very secure and integral but as a user, you can never reach it, then it's terrible in availability which means your system will crash very soon. Accessibility is therefore very important. The way to ensure the best possible availability, we have redundant systems and high availability services, such as systems with multiple links to the outside world. So, we could have two web links. We could have two switch sets and two server sets, so the other one can carry the load if it goes down.

Verification is the next thing we'll think about. So verification is about ensuring that you are the one you claim you are when you ask for permission. The username and password is the most common form of verification, but there are many other forms of authentication. You could use a biometric thumbprint, just as I do when I log in on my Smartphone. Or I have an iPhone X for my wife. She uses her face, another biometric tool. When logging into a secure system with your username and password, you may have a mechanism in which it sends you a code on your e-mail that you must fetch and enter it into the required field to get access to it. This is the form of two-step verification. Some programs like that might give you an SMS code to confirm that you have a mobile phone, something that you have and that you know your login details. Again, this is the whole concept of verification, proof that you tell who you are or it verifies about you. With non-repudiation, we ensure that you say who you are and you can't say you haven't done what you've done.

Non-repudiation is simply about the fact that if you have taken action on a web page; you can't say you haven't done it. There are now many ways to ensure that there is no rejection and most of them are verified properly. For instance, if I want to have a non-repudiation e-mail I've sent to you, I can sign it digitally using my secret key. And if I do it that means no one else would have been able to sign it with that secret key because I am the one who has it. And you know that I sent it, in reality. So you might go and check even if I said that I did not send the message because you have evidence of it. This is the principle of non-repudiation. Again, only the objective of information security management is required for the examination. Also, it aims to protect the information required to carry out the company's business. It is something that you want to ensure that you write it down in your notes and memorize before the examination.

Relationship Management

The next approach is relationship management and you have to learn and memorize the term for the exam. The objective of relations management is to build and foster relationships at tactical and strategic levels between the company and its shareholders. This can be achieved through the detection, evaluation, continuous improvement and supervision of these links among different shareholders. The relation between the supplier and the customer is the most common in these connections. I am the supplier and you are the user/buyer in our relationship. I want to ensure that you're happy, and make sure that all your requirements are met. Therefore, you will be able to crack the test; you'll be satisfied and tell all your friends. So I hope that knowing all this and having a good relationship between us, you can come and try our more books. I have some good things if that happens, resulting from this practice of managing relationships. Now when it comes to tactical and strategic investors, it's not only service providers and consumers, but there are many others involved.

When I'm working through and developing those relationships, I have to identify the expectations of those relationships and manage them as well. What do the investors want exactly? There may be someone who requests a new service or product or they may be interested in something that we already have. As part of the relationship management process, we will speak to our shareholders and find out exactly what are their expectations. Then we can include that in our priorities and work out how we will draw on them. As we do it, we will monitor and guarantee that we achieve all the things we required and then will ensure it is done properly. Then we will pass it again to continuous improvement to make it even better than it used to be. Here again, the whole concept of relationship management at the tactical and strategic level is of the company and its different investors. You will do well if you recall this for the test.

Supplier Management

The last practice you need to remember from the General Management portion is supplier management. You have to recall the concept of supplier management as we discuss it. The aim of this is to ensure that vendors of the company and their output are properly managed to provide smooth, high-quality products, services, and components. We will make sure that we have a strong relationship with our vendors. Thus we can make sure that we develop strong and cooperative ties with these key providers to discover and achieve new values and to reduce our risk of failure. We want to ensure that we have a good relationship if we depend on a certain person for our service, so we can tell when things may not work properly. If we get that, they can come and tell us that you know what? We remember we promised to deliver this service to you this by Tuesday, but we're still behind it, and now it will be before Friday. I would prefer them to tell me now that the thing won't come on Tuesday so I can plan for it. This is the idea of managing suppliers. We will ensure better prices, higher quality products, better service and shipments through good relationships. Again, the goal of the supplier management practice is to ensure that the vendors of the organization and their output are accurately managed to promote the provision of smooth, high-quality products, services and components without interference. Bear that in mind for the test and you can do great things in all questions of vendor management.

Architecture Management

This is another one; you don't have to learn for the ITIL 4 Foundation exam. But we will explain it so that you can grasp it generally. The architectural management practice focuses on the comprehension of all the elements of an organization and the interrelation of these elements, so the organization will be able to achieve its present and future goals successfully. This now offers the organization its principles, norms, and tools to handle the complex transition in a much more organized and agile manner. In your organization, there are five different types of architecture to remember. These include corporate architectures, architectures of the services, architectures of information systems, and technology as well as environment architectures. The business architecture enables a company to analyze its ability to decide how it interacts with the various activities necessary for its business in co-creating value for its clients. Now the architecture of service will provide the organization with an overview of its services and relationships to better understand how they all relate and connect.

This usually leads to the development of a service model and it can be a blueprint or prototype for a variety of organization-wide products. When we consider the architecture of information systems, we focus on the company's conceptual and physical data resources, and their management and distribution to benefit our overall objectives. The technology architecture defines the hardware and software resources required to support the company's service portfolio and products. Let's say, if we use a self-hosted infrastructure for our web servers or if we depend on a cloud-based architecture, we'd fall in this technology architecture paradigm. Finally, environmental architecture describes the external factors affecting our organization and its impact. This model would fit into the environmental design if you recall our discussion of PESTLE earlier. You get the idea of things like politics, the community, social and technological items. All this is outside of our organization, so it is regarded as environmental.

Service management practices

In the Information Technology service management sector, many managed services techniques have been formed over the last 30 years. Within ITIL 4, 17 practices will be in the class of service management. In this section of the book, we will discuss all of them briefly. You now need to learn six of these 17 practical techniques in detail, and four of them at the exam recall stage. During the test, you will need to properly explain how change control, management of incidents, complaint management, help desk, management of resources and management of requests for services operate and work. You need to be able to remember the goals of IT resource management, control and event management, release management and system configuration management activities. Once we have covered the first ten practices, we will go and cover all the remaining practices and they will be covered just for general knowledge, not to learn them for the test. It involves the management of the availability, evaluation of the product, capability and performance management, management of system catalogs, management of business reliability, development of products and service verification and monitoring procedures. However, these procedures will not be on your test.

Change Control

We will discuss change control practices in this chapter. From the exam's perspective, you must be fully aware of this practice. You have to be able to remember its meaning, objective and terminologies and how it functions. So let's continue. Controlling change is basically what we like to call change management. All we need is to make sure that we know who approved the risk and that we handle it on time before we modify it. This is all an act of alignment when we do it. We want to align the positive changes by defending ourselves from the adverse effects of changes. Think of it like this. Whenever you change anything, you risk failure and therefore the change must be worthwhile. We like stable things that work properly, but we also like new features and values and we have to modify it a lot, but that will affect system stability and so we want to manage this risk by managing risk and change control.

Every organization determines the context of change control. This is something that will be determined by the governance, rules, and processes within your business. All IT systems, software, documents, procedures, vendor partnerships and everything else which may directly or indirectly affect a service or product we may alter are included in it. Now I said that you had to learn the meanings of seven terms during the study of our practices. Here is the first one, which is known as a change. A change is now that something that could have a direct or indirect impact on IT infrastructure, which is being introduced, changed or removed. Three different types of modifications exist. These changes are standard, normal and urgent. A standard transition is a preauthorized change. This is something we can do without extra permissions. That is what we always do. The risks are well-identified, which is why there will be little threat. An excellent example would be if someone calls up and demands their password to be changed. This can be done on their own by a service desk consultant.

You need no authorization at all because it is pre-authorized already. It is a simple change that is well understood, but the system continues to change. We consider our second type of change that is normal. These are changes in which approval is to be acquired, but the authorization level is based on the various changes and amount of risk involved in it. Therefore, if it is a small to slightly dangerous thing but we do not regard it as a standard change, the normal process will go through and the person who accepts it is appointed as a change authority. If something is going to be low to medium threat, your manager or boss maybe the person who is change authority. But if you have a big change, then this could be something challenging, it needs a greater degree of permission and will go all the way to a higher authority of change. Again, it will depend on how your company does this, how much tolerance it must risk and how it will be arranged. Allow me to give you a normal change example. For example, you want to update your current system to Windows 2019.

This is a major change so we want to ensure that this transition is properly planned. We want to ensure that the required planning is completed in advance and to ensure that the right permissions are received before the deployment of this new server system. That's the normal change here. We will prepare to schedule accordingly, but it doesn't necessarily mean it's an emergency. Maybe they just failed to prepare so you've got to differentiate between what's an emergency and what's normal, so you should follow the normal process. It's a matter of emergency if anything is damaged and you need the server back up. As I said, a change authority is a person or group who allows the transition. It's normal to have this fragmented in very rapidly moving organizations and we may have several different authorities for change, depending on what's happening.

If you are designing code, the person sitting next to you could potentially be your change authority. You may check and approve their code and they accept your codes. But most of the time, we want to make it much more structured in large companies, and we will follow the normal process of change and have a defined change authority. Now that something from the change authority has been accepted, the transition process moves on. The transition process allows us to plan these changes, to communicate them and to help prevent conflicts and to allocate adequate resources. For example, this week I want to update my website and we'll be down for an hour while we switch servers. So I'm trying to email all my learners in advance so if you're my student, you know that if you try signing in on Tuesday, you can't access it for the time being. This is the principle of setting a changing schedule. We know what will happen now. We will tell you everything ahead of time, and everyone knows that.

It's well organized, pre-planned and well-articulated and I can make sure that my top-level team members are sitting there ready to make changes. So, if something bad happens, there's a list of people who could fix it and make it right. So it affects different aspects of our activities in terms of changing the value as we talk about all this transition. Let's consider we've got a role in our plan. Improvements in our service and product offerings, policies and procedures need a certain degree of control and preparation so that this planning will benefit us with that. We also have many programs for improvement. And when we take initiatives for improvement, we will have to make changes. Let's say, if I want to switch from an older server to a new server, I will use the change control practice as part of the upgrade process. When we speak about involving our clients and users, they should know what changes occur when times are down and can predict the nature of this transition. They need to know what changes take place. Also, we communicate with our clients by sharing it, so we'll use this engage operation. Then these improvements are planned and introduced in certain ways when we look at our design and transformation.

First in design and then into transformation generally because when we accept a change, it will be transitioned to our actual network. Now the change control operation plays a key role in the process of transformation. Then we will get and build stuff. Each time I want to change anything, it means that I buy something new, whether its program or hardware or I build a custom application at home. This all is going into the obtaining and build process. When it's completed, it will be given as an input to this change management practice so that we can approve it and move on to the real servers. And then it comes to the delivery and support eventually. Changes can affect the distribution and maintenance of goods. There can be an enormous impact because if I install a new server, it changes the processes it has. This affects their way of doing things. All that will change. We would also like to ensure that both our clients and staff helping these users undergo improvements. If I don't let the support agents know that we moved from the server of 2011 to the server of 2019 now and that they have no preparation to support 2019, it won't be good so that change makes sure how we care about these kinds of things. We want to ensure that everyone understands the changes that are coming and that we can connect so that everybody is prepared.

Incident Management

This is the next practice we will talk about, and again, you must know this deeply for the exam. Incident management aims at reducing the negative effects of accidents as soon as possible by restoring normal operation. Basically, what will you do if something goes wrong, or drop-in service quality? Each incident must be reported, handled and prioritized according to the defined target response times. The fact that we build our incident management process properly means that we approach it with different incidents from a different angle. I would, therefore, like to take my incidents and classify them according to their different effects. Is this a major accident or a minor incident? Is it an incident of information security or is it an incident of leadership and operations? We need to think about these things as we go through the process of incident management. Now I want to do it based on a negotiated criterion when it comes to giving priority to our incidents. It should be clear to everyone what the criterion is. Will we be using high, medium or low? Will we use a scale of one to five?

Regardless of what it is, the customers will know it, and anyone who follows the program must know it. We should also be able to tell what would a high incident be classified as? What would a small accident be classified as? Is it dollar-based? Is it based on the position of the person in the business? Will it be based on how costly the thing will be? Will it be based on how long we expect it to be down? They are all great ways of classifying it. How your company decides to do this depends very much. You also have to ensure that your incidents that have the greatest business value are addressed first when you give priority to them. It means that if it's anything affecting 100 users or something affecting 10,000 users, we should fix the problem affecting 10,000 users first. It has a greater effect on business. Or if it's a slight inconvenience compared to something that costs you the money, you will get the thing with a price.

Or if it's a slight inconvenience versus something that costs you money, you want to have the thing that is resolved. We now have to use a tool for reporting and managing incidents when it applies to incident management. This is how you can link them with the configuration products, the updates, the various problems, documented errors and others. This also promotes the management of information by having a good program that allows you to handle issues much more easily. One thing they can do for you is that they can compare accidents, other issues and other documented errors with other incidents. For instance, if you call and tell me, that the router in the warehouse is down, this is something I can sign in and it will say, yeah, we have got three more callers in. We know that this is an issue that affects many consumers. The classification should probably go from low to moderate or medium to high. Thus, this is the advantage of a tool for good incident management. Incidents with a greater level of support can be elevated as well.

Perhaps the help desk who will not be the one resolves the accident, will be your first person. If it can't be fixed on its level, it will be elevated to level two supports, and if level two cannot do it will go to level three supports and you will continue before you reach the correct level of support to fix it. This routing will usually be based on the category of the incident. Anyone who works on an incident will bring the reliability and appropriate updates back to this incident management process because your service desk manager is at the forefront as we think about it in the help desk. And then all our technical staff comes. So we can find out how to create a working solution and solve this incident as soon as possible. Furthermore, you might be doing an incident response based on a disaster recovery procedure and if, in this scenario, you would like to join the disaster recovery team because they have the idea of what we are going to do to resolve that disaster. All this will depend on your specific scenario with which you respond. Let's take an example. Maybe a cyber-attack or data-breach is happening in your company.

How can this situation be best handled? Well, I could use a technique called swarming if I and my business is in such danger. It involves bringing together multiple shareholders, all working together initially until it becomes apparent which one of them is better suited in leading and resolving the incident. Once this occurs, we will assign everyone to their appointed roles, and a team leader will take responsibility. The explanation for this is that it brings us all people immediately and this is crucial when you deal with a major incident such as a cyber attack or a loss of records. Perhaps I don't know where that hacker is in the network. Are the databases, the file servers, the web servers involved? I have no idea so I want people working with me from all those departments here. That's why it is called swarming, and then once we know that the attack was on our database, we would then let the file server and web server people go and the database group is still working with us. This is how we want to do this sort of thing. This is how we try to find out how the incidents are better handled.

As we discuss incidents, I want you to focus on the fact that cooperation promotes the sharing of information and training which helps to identify more efficient and effective responses for the incident. This is what we try to do. That's what we do. So which will be useful when we think about this with our operation lens in the value chain? Now let's start with improvement. We should find the incident reports in our incident management process as we speak of change. This is the main input to enhance our operations as we consider the frequency and severity of various incidents, we can find out where we can apply additional manpower, more effort or more money to make ourselves better. Now if we look at that from the engaging operation, we would presume that incidents are apparent to all. Your users will know about it and your clients will know about it so we will have to talk to them in advance and let them know how we resolve these issues and how we know that it is a problem and we will solve it.

If we talk of design and transformation, an incident may occur in a test environment that takes place during development if it occurs. It could also occur during the launch and implementation that is part of the transition. Everything we do we want to make sure that incident control is in position to support us in ensuring the efficient and managed resolution of these incidents. As we think of this from the context of obtaining and building, we want to consider the fact that incidents often happen in development environments. And so things break as I get and build stuff. How do we resolve these issues? There are elements in the field of incident management which can be of use to us, as we want to make sure that we recognize them early before we go into transformation and from transition to delivery and support, to provide and assist in the process. Support and delivery are where we spend plenty of time handling incidents as this benefits our customers greatly. This operation of the value chain provides and facilitates the prevention, detection, and settlement of incidents and issues, and disclosure of them to the user. Now, it leads to our engagement. All of this is important, therefore, for us within the management of incidents. How can we recognize, address, and fix these issues fastly and effectively? That's really what it all gets down to.

Problem Management

This is another one that you must know deeply. I would like you to memorize the objective of problem management for the test. It is to reduce the possibility and effect of incidents by identifying real and potential incident triggers and handling workaround and known errors. There are two main terms that you need to remember for the test in this concept. Those terms are problems and known errors. One or more incidents are caused or potentially caused by a problem. Note that an incident is an accidental service break or a decrease in service quality. It becomes a problem if it occurs more than once in the same thing. However, a problem can sometimes be viewed as a known error. A known error is observed and recognized as a problem that is not yet solved. Let's consider, a website migration from a server to another has recently occurred. We noticed that the access link on our website routes users to the wrong place during this migration. They could not sign in and view their training. We can now inform our users about the problem while our web designer works on resolving the underlying problem.

And we told our users we seemed to have a known error and provided them with a direct connection to a login page access. We have created what is known as a workaround by providing our users with this direct link. A workaround is a method that avoids or eliminates the effect of an incident or problem that does not yet have full resolution. Such workarounds also allow you to minimize the possibility of incidents and they are recorded in the problem reports. Workarounds can be developed at any time and they don't have to wait until you examine the problem thoroughly and have the workable solution done. If a workaround is reported early in the problem-solving process, it can be updated and strengthened upon the conclusion of the problem assessment. We have three main stages inside the product management. The first one is the identification of problems, the second is control of problems, and the third is control of errors. When we consider identifying problems, here's we look at trend analysis stuff. Identify the frequency of repeated incidents or major accidents.

We look at all the details about the manufacturer and the client. The designers of software, prototypes and projects are continuous and detect potential problems that can become issues for us. Throughout our analysis of problem management, we try to evaluate and execute risk-based solutions. We may have a lot of problems, but at the moment we only have enough time and money to solve one. First of all, what should we do? Well, this becomes a judgment on priority selection and risk management. From the viewpoint of all four dimensions, we would also like to do our issue analysis. We want to consider it through all four aspects because this could be an issue that people can solve or vice versa. And then we go into the management of errors. We attempt to identify possible sustainable solutions to this problem through error management. This helps us to reexamine any recognized errors and develop our workarounds so that many of these problems can be resolved.

Problem management is a technique that is also heavily dependent upon other activities. Problems management is overlapping with incident management, risk management, change control, knowledge management and continuous practices for improvement. Each of these practices provides either an input to problem management or receives product management information to do their job better. Now that we talk about problem management and the processes of the value chain, it affects many of them. We will start with the improvement. If we think of improving and effectively managing problems, we will have a better understanding of what we have to do to reduce the number of incidents, thus enhancing our services and products. On the other side, in the engagement process, we must deal with problems that affect our products drastically and inform our clients and consumers about them. If we say something to our customers or consumers, that's a promise which comes under the engaging process.

When we think of this in a design and transformational way, problem-solving will provide information that will help to enhance research and the sharing of expertise by those who develop and implement these products into the real world. And once they reach the real world, your analysts must be aware of this when they offer and support. It's very close to that when we look at it from the context of obtaining and building. Problem-solving exercises will help us identify product issues handled within the overall activity of the value chain, and we want the data to be passed to the transition team as well as distribution and support staff. And we are looking at distribution and support, problem-solving, as incident management, would make a major impact because we can then try to find a timely solution for incidents and resolve them in time by resolving the underlying problem. We want to do this when we dig at the handling of problems. Instead of keep on boasting with every minor incident, we want to find things that happen over and over again and address the root cause and solve it as soon as possible. In the project management process, this is the entire goal here.

Service desk

This is another practice you must be thoroughly aware of. You know most about it because, at some point in our life, most of us approached the service desk. In the service desk practice, demand for resolution of incidents and requests for services are collected. Now, when the service desk receives this issue, request, or inquiry, it is accepted, classified, owned and acted upon. This is the method and procedure which is commonly used for a service desk practice. Now, this is the only argument because you will be able to take everything into your service desk, irrespective of whether it is a request for change, a request for a service or an accident that you can direct to the relevant desk. But this is not the original design for support desks. The service desk's task has changed. Once upon a time, we had a simple service desk to solve technical problems. In modern times, though, it has become the one-stop-shop for consumers and the service provider.

This new focus on the service desk is not just technical problems, but support for individuals and businesses. Our service desk has a big impact on the experience of the user. And so we need to get the right service desk. The service desk is now very critical because of all this. This is one of the first positions for most people to work in the management of IT services. The service desk needs to understand the whole organizational practically and how they work, as they are the gatekeepers. Everything reaches them, and then they must transfer it to the right place. This service desk must be the empathetic connection between the service provider and its users, so you will find it many times, even the most technical people do not work at the desk. Alternatively, the service desk relies on excellent experience with personal contact customer service when the user needs it. Soft skills are really important for service staff compared to technical skills.

Your support and production teams will work closely together with your service desk, transmitting information to and from the service desk, since the service desk must communicate with your clients and understand their desires and demands. When customers call up and ask about the current status of their tickets, they are talking to the service desk, not the technical employee. And so, the technician must ensure that the service desk can communicate the information back to the customer. Now, how does a user access the service desk for support? However, you can count on telephone calls, portals, live to chat with real people, and chatbots, e-Mail, walk-in services, text messages, social media messages or forum boards of discussion. It all relies on how it's going to be done by your company. Four main types of service desks are now available. It is local, centralized, virtual, and follows the sun. In the local service desk, these will be co-located inside or near the customers it supports.

This often helps to interact, provides an individual with a very visible presence and can support a local language or cultural barriers where appropriate. But this is often a great problem because you tie an individual to be in this office and may not have sufficient calls to justify 40 hours of work a week. It is often inefficient and costly. Now, on the other side, a centralized service desk tries to prevent it. Then, you try to put all of the service desk staff in one area and everyone calls a single number from 1 to 800 or goes to some website to receive support all over the world. It requires advanced technology, but it allows us access to calls from all over the world and we can direct those calls to the right agent, regardless of time and day, world-wide. This is what we call virtual service desk: to create a single central service desk through the use of technologies, particularly the Internet and client support devices where staff can be located at any number of locations.

Our fourth model follows the sun, as we call it. Follow the sun is where international companies have two or more geographically distributed service desks that provide 24-hour facilities, follow the sun's coverage. Let's say, we have three service desks services, one in NYC, one in London and another one in India. So, the customer calls would be taken by the London office, since the light of the day is in London. After five hours of gape, the calls would be taken by the New York office. And then in India, they will take calls once it's daylight there. No matter where the customer makes a call, any service desk would be open at the time so that we can cover these three service desks for the full 24 hours. This is the concept here when we're talking about a service desk. We have to ensure that our clients have a location where they can call and receive support whenever they need it. So, how are you operating an efficient service desk? Well, you need technologies which can support your services. This particularly applies to a centralized, virtual or sun desk model.

Such programs may include communication systems, scheduling systems, process control, and resource planning systems, centers of expertise, call and remote access equipment, dashboards and monitoring software, configuration management systems and many more. Then, you have to fill the service desk department up with staff as you put it together. If you hire employees, what should you search for? When you hire staff for the role of service desk, you will look for people with intuition, emotional intelligence, strong communication capabilities, knowledge of company goals, and the ability to perform incident management and prioritization. I did not mention a strong technical ability in that list. Instead, you can say that it can be a technical service desk but it doesn't need to be most of the time. A further focus is on customer care and client service dimensions in many of the sales desks. You can transfer the technical information to the highest level of level support if something goes wrong. Let's explore how the service desk interacts with the operations of the value chain. Improve, first. The operations of the service desk monitor and assess continuously assistance for continuous improvement, standardization and co-creation of value.

They will receive customers ' feedback, gather that and pass that on to the system or method of continuous improvement. The service desk is our main channel for strategic and operational interaction with clients while we think about engagement. They are the people who contact users and talk to them every day. The service desk will provide a forum for engaging with the customers about new and updated products while we speak about design and transformation. Again, the service desk is part of it. So from design and transformation, we'll obtain this data. The employees can also take part in launch preparation, monitoring and early life support. As we talk about obtaining and building, the service desk can also be interested in receiving service items to satisfy service requests like someone has got a problem of crashed hard drive. This is part of obtaining and building. And last but not least, delivery and support. The service desk is centered on this field. The service desk is the coordinating point to handle all incidents, complaints, and demands for services. And so it is very important to get everything right, by ensuring that you have the right people working in your service desk and that they have the proper training and know-how the entire company operates to get the best value for your customers.

Service level management

Management at the service level is something very important and you must learn it deeply. Let's start with its objective first. The aim of the management at the service level is to develop specific business-based goals for service quality to properly evaluate, monitor and manage services delivered against these goals. It will give us end-to-end coverage of the services of the company. It will do this by providing a shared-vision of the services and the desired level of service with clients so that both consumers and we are aware of what to expect. We will also concentrate on gathering, evaluating, processing and documenting the corresponding measures to ensure that service levels are achieved. We also want to ensure that they carry out service level evaluations to ensure that the current services are responsive to customer needs and organization. We will also ensure that we identify and monitor service problems, including quality against our specified levels of service. So when I say I want 95 % throughput, service level management will calculate my performance and see if I reach this point.

All these levels of service will now be defined as an SLA or a service level agreement. A service level agreement is a written service provider-customer arrangement that specifies the necessary services and the expected service rate. This will tell you which standards you have to achieve. The SLA is a method used for measuring the quality of services from a customer perspective. Now, there are a few things you have to do to ensure you have a good SLA. You want to ensure first of all that this is related to a defined service. It cannot be generalized, just as consumers are satisfied. What makes a customer happy? They are happy with the delivery of the email service. They want it to be quick. What does the quickly mean here? You have to ensure that you define the desired outcome, not just operational measurements. Therefore, if the customer demands the quick delivery of the emails, does this mean they're happy when I get it in ten seconds or are they satisfied if I get it there in two minutes? Do I have to be able to define what quickly means?

And I don't only want to do so in terms of output, but also terms of outcomes. We would also like to ensure that our agreement between the service provider and the service customer accurately expresses their opinions. Because if the customer says it should be a fast e-mail service and suggests that two minutes are quick but in this case, the user will believe that it should be simple and that it must take ten seconds to deliver it, so here comes a difference between them. Therefore, we want to be certain that in our agreement we interpret this from the viewpoint of the customer as well as of the users, because that is what SLA really ought to concentrate on, and that is the service users. And the last trick in writing a good SLA is to make sure that you write it in simple words. Make sure it is easy for all groups to understand. This is not a contract; it requires no legal jargon in writing. Instead, make this simple and convenient to understand what you are talking about if someone picks up it. You always want to concentrate on the various relationships when you write your SLAs. This covers relationship management, vendor management, the different expertise and competencies, organizational contacts and business analysts.

These are all aspects that will feed into this Service Level Agreement and make us acknowledge who is accountable for what and at what level. The management of our services is now focused on these different information sources, like our SLA. This is our engagement with the client and our partnership. We have other things like our client engagement so that we can listen to the demands of our clients. We find and collect information they like to know about us. We want to have the assessment and discussions on the iterative process with them. We would also like to ask simple questions open to the public. Through collecting this information from our service desk or client contacts, we will learn a great deal of information and develop a good management service level plan. We want to receive feedback from customers later. It might look like a survey or important measurements and metrics related to the company. We might focus on other operating metrics, such as server throughput and capacity in your organization. Or we might focus on some market metrics, for example, annual recurring revenue or a customer's lifelong value. All that can be provided as an input into this process in this service level management.

Now that we look at it and see how it impacts our operation in the value chain, let us discuss the behavior of the program i.e, plan activity. Your management of the services will help your service and product portfolio preparation and service offerings through planning activities because all the data about the actual performance of the products and trends will be part of this entire plan. If you look at this from an improvement perspective, management of the service level will allow us to constantly enhance and improve our services. When we discussed the different stages of the continuous improvement model, you have seen it. We had to evaluate things and see if we achieved those goals. This is known as SLM. We talk about engagement here. Service level management guarantees that through feedback procedures we are constantly working with our clients and our users and we receive information from them for continuous analysis. Now that we talk about it from a transformation and design point of view, the management of service level is an insight into designing and developing new services. If the client wants quick e-mail delivery that is less than ten seconds, then we have to build a system that satisfies this requirement and this will be an input to the process.

To obtain and build, service level management includes component and system quality goals and evaluation and monitoring abilities for the products and services that we use. The obtaining and building process in the service level management should receive a lot of input information. Lastly, we come to delivery and support. Service level management explains to the management and support staff the goals of service quality so that they know what they want to achieve. It will also gather information and recommendations from them to provide input into the management of service levels and service enhancements we will make in the future. So it works like that. All of these measurements and metrics contribute to service level management. We establish the right criteria, interact with the consumer and ensure that we measure the right things and see whether we follow such criteria.

Service request management

We are discussing our practice of service request management in this section. The goal of the service request management process is to facilitate the agreed services performance through the efficient and user-friendly handling of all approved service requests submitted by the user. Now such service demands have been pre-defined and pre-agreed. Let's say, to create a new email address for delivery there is a standard process and a standard request approach. Or you might need an earphone set for you to attach at work to your device. Again, this could be a service request. Perhaps you'd like to go from a 15 "computer screen to a 21" screen. Again, this could be a standard request for service. Essentially, three sections are included in the standard service request; you have initiation, acceptance, and fulfillment. Currently, service demands are usually included in the service delivery and are not used for service loss or deterioration which is used for handling incidents. Alternatively, service requests require normal things, things we require. I need more drive storage, additional e-mail accounts, other e-mail addresses, opening my password.

All these things are requests and demands from our services. A service request is essentially a demand by an authorized user or a representative of a user requesting a service action decided as part of the normal service delivery. Service demand can be fulfilled by changing products or their elements and is typically a standard modification because they are at minimal risk and understandable. Many cases of these would include a demand for a service delivery operation, such as getting a new device for the new employee. It could be an information request. It could be a resource or a software provision request. Instead of 10 gigabytes, give me 20 gigabytes of storage. It may be a request that a resource or service is accessible. Or you could say, I now need access to the share accounting drive because I'm just moving here. These are some good examples. And feedbacks, positive comments, and objections can also be available in here.

All these must follow the procedure of the service request. Service requirements and their fulfillment should always, as further as possible, be streamlined and automated. Such factors are again low-risk things; you need to do them as much as possible with a program of self-help so that you are not tying good people together with those standard service demands requiring full-time equal man-hours. Alternatively, we want to preserve some man-hours or full-time events with which we have to deal with such incidents. Within the service request method, there are many possibilities for improvement. You should always define them and then incorporate them to ensure quicker fulfillment rates and use automation and benefit from it whenever possible. It encourages you to ensure that your guidelines are properly established and that your demands are met with minimal or no extra permissions if you have appropriate policies. So that we can simplify fulfillment, optimize it and automate processes. It reduces the cost to a minimum and ensures that customers get what they want as soon as possible. This way of doing things is great.

Therefore, consumers ' requirements of fulfillment periods must be clearly defined and implemented based on what the business would deliver. Let's say, when you purchase a coupon from a site, for example, my website I tell you that you can access a 28 "monitor screen. It may involve some cost so you cannot have that acceptance alone. Then, you just requested that service which goes to your supervisor who then accepts the financial part of it. And, perhaps I want access to the finance share drive. That's a security issue with information so someone from the finance department will allow doing that. Management of a service request would focus, as I have been thinking about, on well-specified processes and procedures. The more you can use it, the more you can control all of these demands and optimize them to reduce their labor force. Your service requests may include basic workflows or very complicated workflows; this depends on how you want to do it, which improvements and permissions are to be made there, depending on your organization. You want to ensure all measures are well-known and confirmed to satisfy these requests. You tried it, managed to make it functional, streamlined it, and then automated it.

Your supplier can always agree to fulfillment periods and give its users a clear status. You want to ensure that you always use this engaged arch to tell the clients what you want. If you are smart enough to give them the expectation of when it should be, that will help to clarify much of the uncertainty and the fear your clients may have. If you talk about your service request, note that many can be achieved by an experience of self-service. Factors like resetting passwords, requesting additional space on the shared drive, most of them can be fully automated. Consider automation when you are handling service requests. I hope this lesson you heard me say it a lot, but it's very important inside this. Also, wherever possible, I want you to utilize the current workflow templates so that you needn't start to build things from scratch. Whenever you have something, even if it's a manual process of fulfillment, look at it; how do you simplify it, and then how do you automate it? And I know that we have discussed a lot in the management of service requests, but from the viewpoint of the value chain, we will talk about them now. How are we going to relate as we talk about improving it?

In this situation, the management of service requests can provide us with the platform of initiatives to change. We can get our customers ' feedback and suggestions and then add to the cycle of improvement to find these patterns and to see if it can be better in the future. If we look at it from the viewpoint of engagement we want to see that the management of service requests requires frequent interactions to tell users what they can expect. What are the needs, priorities, and status? When we think of this from the viewpoint of design and transformation, we have these regular improvements to the products we demand, and we begin to initiate and fulfill these as service requests. To obtain and build, it must be fulfilled if I ask for something. And it will be fulfilled, which means that we may have to purchase, acquire or build something under the production process, so that's we're doing it like tying it up to this service. And then we're talking delivery and support eventually. The management of service requests contributes significantly to our normal service delivery because this operation shows our users everything we can do for them and encourages them to ask for them. Perhaps you would like to have a wider screen, more drive space to share, a new user profile. We can do all these things and guarantee that users can receive what they need to produce and to ensure that we satisfy all their requirements criteria. That's what service management demands are about, meaning that consumers get what they need to achieve to operate to high efficiency.

IT Asset management

In this chapter, we will discuss IT asset management practices. And this ends with those of which we will only learn from the recall. And what you need to know about this lesson is to memorize IT asset management purposes. It includes scheduling and controlling the entire life cycle of IT assets to help the company optimize value, control costs, managing risk, support purchasing decision-making, recycle and removal of assets, and fulfill compliance and contractual obligations. But you must memorize the word IT resource that was used in that purpose along with its purpose. So, IT asset refers to what type of things? It is any useful IT resource that will contribute to IT service or product distribution. Now when we talk of IT asset management, the fact that it is like a stock is what I want you to think of. We want to know all the elements within our enterprise and what they do for us because I can help maximize benefits as I know all of them. It can help me to control the cost. I will handle risks.

And I can help in future purchasing decision-making. So if I take my company's example, we have a lot of computers we use here. So, I have to watch the computers and how old are they because I know that I have to replace them every three years. This will cost me an x dollar figure. We must, therefore, start budgeting. The management of IT assets benefits us in this situation. It allows us to schedule and controls the whole life cycle from sales to the removal and substitution of these IT assets. Here's the entire concept. Again, a value-added element or resource can be taken as an IT asset. It's one of our IT assets that help to deliver an IT product or service. These could be cell phones. These could include the servers, the infrastructure of the network, cabinets, switches, printers, computers, tablets, desktops and monitors, whatever you name it, it is an IT asset.

Asset management is one of the staff members, who walk around with a checklist, who writes model numbers and observes the software installed on each computer without any strong IT asset management software. It is difficult even to start collecting details like software licenses were updated without a lot of frustration and intensive effort if that is the point where you're in asset management. It is because IT asset management is an essential component of ITIL. This offers the mechanism for documenting and maintaining each IT asset's lifecycle when it is first asked to remove the asset and every step in between. If the service desk provides information about each IT asset and where it exists, IT staff can provide service consistency and control service costs more efficiently. If you are following the ITIL lifecycle or at least using some of the best practices, a reliable IT asset management program like this will help you succeed.

ITIL asset management has as its priorities, the obtaining of suitable IT assets while maintaining low cost and high profits, the optimization of the use of each IT asset, IT asset removal when the cost of maintenance surpasses their benefits, the supply of information needed to comply with the regulations, license rehabilitation and renewal contracts. An ITIL asset management system allows better management of incidents and issues by supplying important asset knowledge for IT service desk staff. This can increase settlement rates and ensure fast maintenance time. The link of service information to individual assets often helps to pass, attach or change configurations. And a good asset management program allows the monitoring of software licenses and guarantees to prevent unnecessary maintenance costs or fines for violations of license terms. It helps to reduce the expense of IT service management

IT asset management advantages: it is important to understand where an IT asset is, the financial aspects associated with it and its current state such as it is operating, retired or recovered. In the meantime, you need to also learn its configuration, upgrade, shift, and link to your network. That, therefore, requires information that nurtures the management of both assets and configuration. In theory, where redundant instruments, distinct databases, and IT asset recovery are available, a business could eliminate costs together with overall better ownership and return on investment management. In many organizations, the traditional and siloed mindset has always influenced asset management and efficient service delivery. We need the service value system to look at these components for ITIL 4.

ITIL 4 has now accepted IT asset management as a vital service management practice. Although one was from the procurement/finance and the other was from IT, there was a desire to mix the idea of asset management with configuration management earlier. However, ITIL 4 describes them as two distinct practices a crucial step in the right way when defining the incentives that each practice offers. Asset management examines the transition of what an IT asset is, for instance, a smart refrigerator is an IT asset in our technology. It also explores the purpose of bringing an asset to a company, its advantages, interest, cost, and exposure; what its depletion is and how do you treat it from a support perspective? All of this has to do with the asset management but how you use this resource to offer a service is where ITIL 4 inventory and service setup comes in.

Conclusion

In this book, we've achieved and learned a lot of things. And I want to put everything together in this section. We have discussed the four aspects of service management, including organization and people, the information and technology market, stakeholders and vendors, and then the value chain and operations. Then we discussed the Service Value System of ITIL framework. It involved our possibilities and demands as an input, and those are formed by our company's Service Value Chain, governance, procedures, guiding principles and continuous improvement. And we have a value from the other side. As part of the service value system, we have dived into the service value chain itself. We also studied its various parts such as engaging, planning, improvement, design, and transformation, obtaining and building, delivery and support, then our services and products. After that, we have spent the last three phases of this book discussing 34 separate ITIL 4 practices. However, now is the moment for us to bring everything together. Let us now go through a real-life scenario and see how everything we have discussed till now is translated into the required value.

Let us now assume that we are working for a big logistics company such as Amazon or Walmart. And within the corporation, we are part of their organization of IT services management. They have a warehouse with Wi-Fi to give the lift truck driver the right directions on his cell phone that tells him which alley and rack the package he has to pick up. However, in this zone of the warehouse, the wireless connection enabling Wi-Fi is not working properly. And the mobile phone of the driver cannot obtain the information he needs. This has a major impact on our business, now that if the driver cannot get the guidelines fast enough, it risks missing an important business deadline. After all, certain businesses such as Amazon focus on extremely-fast shipping as a core business model feature. Although this may look relatively simple, the steps of a prearranged incident management protocol cannot be handled by merely following them. There are many interconnections between this wireless network's practices and operations to be resolved and to return to the normal services.

So, first, let's continue with the process of the service value system. First, we'll see we've got a request as a demand. And in this situation, the manager of that specific warehouse and the lift truck driver notice that the Wi-Fi service doesn't work very well in a certain area of the warehouse. This indicates that the lift truck driver must return to the boss's office in deliveries and figure out where his next order is inside the warehouse. This leads to delays and could miss the target dates of deliveries. It's an incident. They now shift from this demand to the engagement process in which the manager of the warehouse must call up the service desk. The desk officer listens to the query that the warehouse manager presents. They report it into the incident management process and mark it as a high priority. The officer will then let the warehouse manager know that the issue will be extended to the wireless network technical support team. And every three hours they give updates until the problem is resolved. Now, the service desk officer is expanding to bring it to the wireless network support team for the wireless connection.

These are the people with the delivery and support role for this wireless network in the value chain operation. It helps the service desk office to provide the support engineer with the details, and this engineer can start with the diagnosis and examination of the incident. The support engineer for the network then recognizes the failure of that wireless access point. Then he wants to replace it with a substitute from the warehouse of current replacement parts. There will be several practices in this operation alone. First, we have the IT asset management method to check and update the serial number of the database of the configuration item. Then he undergoes the practice for configuration management because he must configure and install this device based on the approval. He will also go through the process of change control as he will add a new device into the network. Of course, as he focuses on handling an incident, he will go through the incident control process. Suppose the substitution is seen as a normal improvement for this wireless access point.

There is, therefore, no need for further approvals. If it were a normal adjustment, we would pass to the change management process and get permission from it or intensify it as a matter of emergency. But, in any case, all this would arise in the discipline of change control practice. Eventually, our network engineer installs the access point, ensures it functions and monitors the management system for incidents. Afterward, he contacts the service desk officer and informs him that the incident is over. Now that it's solved, the engineer sits back and comments on what has happened. And he's concerned about other ways he can more effectively repair this. If he finds any other solution, he can add them as recommendations for future developments in the continuous improvements register. When he does that, it becomes part of the continuous improvement process and improve activity. Now, on the other hand, the desk officer contributes to the engagement operation by interacting with the warehouse manager. Then he informs them that the wireless network should be functioning again. He asks the manager to ensure that the cell phone of the lift truck driver functions again and he is informed by this.

And he can close the accident absolutely when he does this. So, when we discuss this service value system's final component, we get value. The value is co-created by making a return to the wireless coverage, and the lift truck driver can now again do his job more effectively using that cell phone to find where the items he wants to pick and transport are to be found. About one hour later, the warehouse management will receive a short email demanding an investigation of user satisfaction. This could require his feedback and resolution of the incident. It'd become another engagement activity. Okay, once he finishes the survey, we will take it and we can define patterns and trends based on satisfaction ratings and users ' comments based on the data received. This would come under our area of improvement. And we will decide if we work effectively with our incident management program and our procedures. So, it's been much. As you have seen, all this connects, and throughout this single incident and this resolution, we engage in and leave various activities and practices.

It's not just a linear process. But instead, during this quick example, we moved from the engagement process to delivery and support, back to engage, and then goes over to improvement, and many other practices, multiple times. Note, it is the key to create and promote good service management to recognize and understand all these interconnections. You have to remember all these aspects when you focus on one of your processes or at one of your workflows when you set it out.

Practice Test

Question: "Four Ps" of Service design are Partners, People, Processes and ___.

(a) Profession

(b) Preparation

(c) Products

(d) Potential

Question: What is the best way to describe an incident?

(a) An unplanned disruption of service unless there is a backup to that service

(b) Any unplanned disruption

(c) Any disruption to service that is reported to the service desk, regardless of whether the service is impacted or not

(d) An unplanned interruption to service or a reduction in the quality of service

Question: The best way to describe Hierarchic escalation is:

(a) Failing to meet the incident resolution times specified in a service level agreement

(b) Passing an incident to people with a greater level of technical skill

(c) Notifying more senior levels of management about an incident

(d) Using more senior specialists than necessary to resolve an Incident to maintain customer satisfaction

Question: Which process deals with complaints, comments, and general enquiries from users?

(a) Service portfolio management

(b) Demand management

(c) Request fulfilment

(d) Service level management

Question: What are customers of IT services who work in the same organization as the service provider known as?

(a) External customers

(b) Internal customers

(c) Strategic customers

(d) Valued customers

Question: Which is the correct definition of a customer facing service?

(a) One which is not covered by a service level agreement

(b) A service that cannot be allowed to fail

(c) One which directly supports the business processes of customers

(d) A service not directly used by the business

Question: Which one of the following is the CORRECT set of steps for the continual service improvement approach?

(a) Devise a strategy; Design the solution; Transition into production; Operate the solution; Continually improve

(b) Where do we want to be? How do we get there?; How do we check we arrived?; How do we keep the momentum going?

(c) Identify the required business outcomes; Plan how to achieve the outcomes; Implement the plan; Check the plan has been properly implemented; Improve the solution

(d) What is the vision?; Where are we now?; Where do we want to be?; How do we get there?; Did we get there?; How do we keep the momentum going?

Question: Which one of the following contains information that is passed to service transition to enable the implementation of a new service?

(a) A service option

(b) A service charter

(c) A service transition package (STP)

(d) A service design package (SDP)

Question: Which of the following BEST describes service strategies value to the business?

(a) Allows higher volumes of successful change

(b) Enabling the service provider to have a clear understanding of what levels of service will make their customers successful

(c) Reduction in unplanned costs through optimized handling of service outages

(d) Reduction in the duration and frequency of service outages

Question: What are the categories of event described in the UIL service operation book?

(a) Informational, scheduled, normal

(b) Informational, warning, exception

(c) Scheduled, unscheduled, emergency

(d) Warning, reactive, proactive

Question: Who is responsible for ensuring that the request fulfillment process is being performed according to the agreed and documented standard?

(a) The service owner

(b) The process owner

(c) The customer

(d) The IT director

Question: Which process will perform risk analysis and review of all suppliers and contracts on a regular basis?

(a) The service level management

(b) The service catalogue management

(c) The supplier management

(d) The IT service continuity management

Question: Which process is responsible for providing the rights to use an IT service?

(a) Incident management

(b) Request fulfillment

(c) Change management

(d) Access management

Question: Which of the following options is a hierarchy that is used in knowledge management?

(a) Knowledge - Wisdom - Information - Data

(b) Data - Information - Knowledge – Wisdom

(c) Information - Data - Knowledge - Wisdom

(d) Wisdom - Information - Data - Knowledge

Question: Which one of the following would NOT be defined as part of every process?

(a) Functions

(b) Metrics

(c) Inputs and outputs

(d) Roles

Question: Which one of the following is NOT part of the service design stage of the service lifecycle?

(a) Producing quality, secure and resilient designs for new or improved services

(b) Measuring the effectiveness and efficiency of service design and the supporting processes

(c) Designing and maintaining all necessary service transition packages

(d) Taking service strategies and ensuring they are reflected in the service design processes and the service designs that are produced

Question: Which process is responsible for discussing reports with customers showing whether services have met their targets?

(a) Continual service improvement

(b) Service level management

(c) Change management

(d) Availability management

Question: Which of the following is an objective of business relationship management?

(a) To secure funding to manage the provision of services

(b) To ensure high levels of customer satisfaction

(c) To ensure strategic plans for IT services exist

(d) To identify patterns of business activity

Question: Which process includes business, service and component sub-processes?

(a) Financial management

(b) Service level management

(c) Capacity management

(d) Incident management

Question: Which two processes will contribute MOST to enabling effective problem detection?

(a) Change and release and deployment management

(b) Incident and financial management

(c) Incident and event management

(d) Knowledge and service level management

Question: Where would you expect incident resolution targets to be documented?

(a) A service description

(b) A service level agreement (SLA)

(c) A request for change (RFC)

(d) The service portfolio

Question: Which one of the following is an objective of service catalogue management?

(a) Negotiating and agreeing service level agreement

(b) Ensuring that the service catalogue is made available to those approved to access it

(c) Negotiating and agreeing operational level agreements

(d) Only ensuring that adequate technical resources are available

Question: What type of baseline captures the structure, contents and details of the infrastructure and represents a set of items that are related to each other?

(a) Configuration baseline

(b) Project baseline

(c) Change baseline

(d) Asset baseline

Question: How many people should be accountable for a process as defined in the RACI model?

(a) Only one - the process architect

(b) As many as necessary to complete the activity

(c) Two - the process owner and the process enactor

(d) Only one - the process owner

Question: Which process is responsible for the availability, confidentiality and integrity of data?

(a) Service asset and configuration management

(b) Information security management

(c) Service catalogue management

(d) Change management

Question: Which one of the following is concerned with policy and direction?

(a) Capacity management

(b) Service design

(c) Governance

(d) Service level management

Question: Service transition contains detailed descriptions of which processes?

(a) Change management, service asset and configuration management, release and deployment management

(b) Service asset and configuration management, release and deployment management, request fulfillment

(c) Change management, capacity management event management, service request management

(d) Service level management, service portfolio management, service asset and configuration management

Question: Understanding what to measure and why it is being measured are key contributors to which part of the Service Lifecycle?

(a) Service Operation

(b) Service Design

(c) Service Strategy

(d) Continual Service Improvement

Question: Which one of the following is the BEST definition of the term service management?

(a) A set of specialized organizational capabilities for providing value to customers in the form of services

(b) A group of interacting, interrelated, or independent components that form a unified whole, operating together for a common purpose

(c) The management of functions within an organization to perform certain activities

(d) Units of organizations with roles to perform certain activities

Question: The consideration of value creation is a principle of which stage of the service lifecycle?

(a) Service design

(b) Service transition

(c) Continual service improvement

(d) Service strategy

Question: What would you call the groups of people who have an interest in the activities, targets, resources and deliverables from service management?

(a) Regulators

(b) Stakeholders

(c) Employers

(d) Accreditors

Question: What are underpinning contracts used to document?

(a) Metrics and critical success factors (CSFs) for internal support teams

(b) The provision of goods and services by third party suppliers

(c) Service levels that have been agreed between the internal service provider and their customer

(d) The provision of IT services or business services by a service provider

Question: Which of the following is NOT one of the five individual aspects of service design?

(a) The design of the technology architectures

(b) The design of market spaces

(c) The design of new or changed services

(d) The design of the service portfolio, including the service catalogue

Question: Which of these statements about resources and capabilities is CORRECT?

(a) Resources are types of service asset and capabilities are not

(b) Capabilities are types of service asset and resources are not

(c) Resources and capabilities are both types of service asset

(d) Neither capabilities nor resources are types of service asset

Question: What body exists to support the authorization of changes and to assist change management in the assessment and prioritization of changes?

(a) The change advisory board

(b) The change authorization board

(c) The change implementer

(d) The change manager

Question: Which of the following is NOT a recognized example of a service provider type within the ITIL framework?

(a) Shared services unit

(b) Internal

(c) External

(d) Service desk

Question: Which one of the following can help determine the level of impact of a problem?

(a) Statement of requirements (SOR)

(b) Definitive media library (DML)

(c) Standard operating procedures (SOP)

(d) Configuration management system (CMS)

Question: The effective management of risk requires specific types of action. Which of the following pairs of actions would be BEST to manage risk?

(a) Training in risk management for all staff and identification of risks

(b) Identification of risk, analysis and management of the exposure to risk

(c) Control of exposure to risk and investment of capital

(d) Training of all staff and investment of capital

Question: Which of the following BEST describes the purpose of access management?

(a) To prevent problems and resulting Incidents from happening

(b) Provides the rights for users to be able to use a service or group of services

(c) To detect security events and make sense of them

(d) To provide a channel for users to request and receive standard services

Question: Which process will regularly analyze incident data to identify discernible trends?

(a) Event management

(b) Service level management

(c) Problem management

(d) Change management

Question: Which one of the following includes four stages called Plan, Do, Check and Act?

(a) The continual service improvement approach

(b) The service lifecycle

(c) The Deming Cycle

(d) The seven-step improvement process

Question: What type of services are NOT directly used by the business but are required by the service provider to deliver customer facing services?

(a) Customer services

(b) Component services

(c) Business services

(d) Supporting services

Question: Which process is responsible for ensuring that appropriate testing takes place?

(a) Service level management

(b) Knowledge management

(c) Release and deployment management

(d) Service asset and configuration management

Practice Test Answers

Question: "Four Ps" of Service design are Partners, People, Processes and ___.

(c) Products (Correct)

Question: What is the best way to describe an incident?

(d) An unplanned interruption to service or a reduction in the quality of service (Correct)

Question: The best way to describe Hierarchic escalation is:

(c) Notifying more senior levels of management about an incident (Correct)

Question: Which process deals with complaints, comments, and general enquiries from users?

(c) Request fulfilment (Correct)

Question: What are customers of IT services who work in the same organization as the service provider known as?

(b) Internal customers (Correct)

Question: Which is the correct definition of a customer facing service?

(c) One which directly supports the business processes of customers (Correct)

Question: Which one of the following is the CORRECT set of steps for the continual service improvement approach?

(d) What is the vision?; Where are we now?; Where do we want to be?; How do we get there?; Did we get there?; How do we keep the momentum going? (Correct)

Question: Which one of the following contains information that is passed to service transition to enable the implementation of a new service?

(d) A service design package (SDP) (Correct)

Question: Which of the following BEST describes service strategies value to the business?

(b) Enabling the service provider to have a clear understanding of what levels of service will make their customers successful (Correct)

Question: What are the categories of event described in the UIL service operation book?

(b) Informational, warning, exception (Correct)

Question: Who is responsible for ensuring that the request fulfillment process is being performed according to the agreed and documented standard?

(b) The process owner (Correct)

Question: Which process will perform risk analysis and review of all suppliers and contracts on a regular basis?

(c) The supplier management (Correct)

Question: Which process is responsible for providing the rights to use an IT service?

(d) Access management (Correct)

Question: Which of the following options is a hierarchy that is used in knowledge management?

(b) Data - Information - Knowledge – Wisdom (Correct)

Question: Which one of the following would NOT be defined as part of every process?

(a) Functions (Correct)

Question: Which one of the following is NOT part of the service design stage of the service lifecycle?

(c) Designing and maintaining all necessary service transition packages (Correct)

Question: Which process is responsible for discussing reports with customers showing whether services have met their targets?

(b) Service level management (Correct)

Question: Which of the following is an objective of business relationship management?

(b) To ensure high levels of customer satisfaction (Correct)

Question: Which process includes business, service and component sub-processes?

(c) Capacity management (Correct)

Question: Which two processes will contribute MOST to enabling effective problem detection?

(c) Incident and event management (Correct)

Question: Where would you expect incident resolution targets to be documented?

(b) A service level agreement (SLA) (Correct)

Question: Which one of the following is an objective of service catalogue management?

(b) Ensuring that the service catalogue is made available to those approved to access it (Correct)

Question: What type of baseline captures the structure, contents and details of the infrastructure and represents a set of items that are related to each other?

(a) Configuration baseline (Correct)

Question: How many people should be accountable for a process as defined in the RACI model?

(d) Only one - the process owner (Correct)

Question: Which process is responsible for the availability, confidentiality and integrity of data?

(b) Information security management (Correct)

Question: Which one of the following is concerned with policy and direction?

(c) Governance (Correct)

Question: Service transition contains detailed descriptions of which processes?

(a) Change management, service asset and configuration management, release and deployment management (Correct)

Question: Understanding what to measure and why it is being measured are key contributors to which part of the Service Lifecycle?

(d) Continual Service Improvement (Correct)

Question: Which one of the following is the BEST definition of the term service management?

(a) A set of specialized organizational capabilities for providing value to customers in the form of services (Correct)

Question: The consideration of value creation is a principle of which stage of the service lifecycle?

(d) Service strategy (Correct)

Question: What would you call the groups of people who have an interest in the activities, targets, resources and deliverables from service management?

(b) Stakeholders (Correct)

Question: What are underpinning contracts used to document?

(b) The provision of goods and services by third party suppliers (Correct)

Question: Which of the following is NOT one of the five individual aspects of service design?

(b) The design of market spaces (Correct)

Question: Which of these statements about resources and capabilities is CORRECT?

(c) Resources and capabilities are both types of service asset (Correct)

Question: What body exists to support the authorization of changes and to assist change management in the assessment and prioritization of changes?

(a) The change advisory board (Correct)

Question: Which of the following is NOT a recognized example of a service provider type within the ITIL framework?

(d) Service desk (Correct)

Question: Which one of the following can help determine the level of impact of a problem?

(d) Configuration management system (CMS) (Correct)

Question: The effective management of risk requires specific types of action. Which of the following pairs of actions would be BEST to manage risk?

(b) Identification of risk, analysis and management of the exposure to risk (Correct)

Question: Which of the following BEST describes the purpose of access management?

(b) Provides the rights for users to be able to use a service or group of services (Correct)

Question: Which process will regularly analyze incident data to identify discernible trends?

(c) Problem management (Correct)

Question: Which one of the following includes four stages called Plan, Do, Check and Act?

(c) The Deming Cycle (Correct)

Question: What type of services are NOT directly used by the business but are required by the service provider to deliver customer facing services?

(d) Supporting services (Correct)

Question: Which process is responsible for ensuring that appropriate testing takes place?

(c) Release and deployment management (Correct)

Have courage in your heart and a calm mind. Surely you would do well. Good luck for your ITILv4 certification exam.

www.ingramcontent.com/pod-product-compliance
Lightning Source LLC
Chambersburg PA
CBHW080539060326
40690CB00022B/5172